Whymper's Scrambles with a Camera
A Victorian magic lantern show

Peter Berg

Peter Berg

Dedicated to the memory of Edward Whymper,
mountaineer, artist and writer 1840 - 1911

15.V.13

Edward Whymper as a young man

Whymper's Scrambles with a Camera

A Victorian magic lantern show

Peter Berg
Former Hon. Archivist The Alpine Club

With a foreword by
Stephen Venables
Former President The Alpine Club

First published in Great Britain in 2011 by the
Alpine Club 55/56 Charlotte Road London EC2A 3QT

Cover photographs taken from Whymper's illustrations
Front cover: Edward Whymper as a young man
Matterhorn and Hornli
A cannonade on the Matterhorn
Mutual Assistance
Dragon appears again
Matterhorn from the Theodule

Back cover: Boden Glacier
Janssen ascending

Typeset in Garamond from the author's word processor
by Michelle Smythe at idesign, Kendal

Book designed by John Slee-Smith

Printed in England by the Stramongate Press, Kendal, Cumbria

British Library cataloguing Data. A catalogue record for this book is available from the British Library

ISBN 978-0-900523-67-0

Contents

Foreword

by Steven Venables, President of the Alpine Club 2005-2007

Edward Whymper was an anachronism: a talented engraver who despised the romanticism of Ruskin and Turner; an earnest man of trade elected to join the urbane dons, lawyers and clergymen who made up the nascent Alpine Club; a determinedly commercial professional mountaineer in an age of lofty amateurism.

As Peter Berg points out in his introduction, Whymper was inspired at the age of eighteen by Albert Smith performing his celebrated lecture on the ascent of Mont Blanc. Smith, a flashy entertainer with virtually no climbing experience, was a bit of charlatan, peddling a travesty of the real thing; he was the Victorian forerunner of today's instant celebrity Everest summiteers. Whymper, when he came to deliver *his* first lecture, just three years after hearing Smith, was already establishing himself as the genuine article. As a mountaineer he was canny, ambitious and skilful. He also had enormous stamina, as Peter Berg reminds us here, with mention of the famous 70 miles walk from Briançon to Grenoble in just 18 hours. In driving rain.

The Matterhorn was Whymper's overriding obsession and it made him a household name. However, it's worth pointing out that, during the three weeks before his first ascent of the mountain 1865, Whymper and his guides walked several hundred miles through the Alps, making first ascents, en route, of the Grand Cornier, the Grandes Jorasses, the Aiguille Verte and the Ruinette, as well as first crossings of the Portons Pass, Col de Talèfre and Col Dolent. The last of these involved *descending* a fifty degrees ice face.

As Whymper's first biographer, Frank Smythe, observed, 'To Whymper a mountaineering holiday meant continuous activity, and rest days, instead of being pleasant oases in which the beauty of the heights might be viewed in philosophic calm, from a flower-clad alp or meadow, were merely disagreeable hiatuses of forced inactivity.' Smythe may have had a less austere attitude to rest days, but he too was a determined professional, with a gift for communicating his pastime to a wide public. In more recent times, Chris Bonington has been the consummate master in that field. But Whymper was the first to combine genuine mountaineering accomplishment with popular appeal.

Scrambles Amongst the Alps has never been out of print. The writing is vivid and assured, with flashes of humour that belie the earnest pomposity Whymper displayed as a younger man in his diary. The book was illustrated, of course, with Whymper's own splendidly melodramatic engravings. Those images have been associated indelibly with the man for nearly a century and a half. Far less familiar are the *photographs* – some of the very first mountain photographs – he used to illustrate his public lantern lectures. What a pleasure it is to see those pictures reproduced, as Whymper presented them, for the first time since his death.

What this re-creation of Whymper's lecture makes clear is that it was not a mere record of climbing achievement aimed at climbing geeks: even if he was a proper mountaineer's mountaineer, Whymper aimed to entertain a much wider audience. His lecture is as much about the culture, people and mountains of the Alps, as it is about his own achievements. The magnificent photos must have stunned contemporary audiences, for whom the alpine landscape was still a novelty. A century and a half later, they remain stunning images, perhaps now *more* remarkable for showing us how much that landscape has changed. It is fascinating to see the villages of the Zermatt valley as they were a century and a half ago, heart-warming to witness Whymper's admiration for the great guides like Croz, Anderegg and Zurbriggen. It is also slightly melancholic to observe just how magnificent the glaciers were then, compared to their shrivelled, desiccated appearance now. At a time when the Alps – and alpinism – are changing very fast, this is a fascinating recreation of what really was a pioneering 'Golden Age' of mountaineering.

Acknowledgements

First of all I have to thank Glyn Hughes, then Hon Sec of the AC, for inviting me, back in 1995, to do some research on the lantern slides in the club's collections, attributed to Edward Whymper. After the results of this work were published in the AJ in 1997, George Band encouraged me to recreate the lecture, delivered in 1998 on the occasion of the presentation of EW's ice axe to the club. The book was longer in appearing, but with the support of the then AC President, Paul Braithwaite, and an informal committee of wise club members consisting of Henry Day, Anna Lawford, Hywel Lloyd, Jerry Lovatt and John Cleare (who also did heroic work on the captions), it will come out in 2011 to commemorate the centenary of EW's death.

Other AC members have been helpful in many ways: Ian Smith, sharing information obtained while preparing his forthcoming biography of EW (and his partner Eleanor for a picture of the Whymper family home); David Baldock for help with the pictures; and, more than anyone else, John Slee-Smith for his tremendous work in turning a rough draft into a book. And I feel greatly honoured that Steven Venables, our former President and distinguished climber, writer and lecturer on mountaineering, agreed to write a Foreword.

Outside the club, I've had help from members of the Whymper family, the guides Antonio Carrel of Valtournenche and Jean-Yves Frederiksen of Abondance, the National Media Museum in Bradford, the Scott Polar Research Institute in Cambridge, the Magic Lantern Society, current and past Ilford employees, the Visitor Information Centre in Haslemere and many others.

And I wish to record a special debt to the late Peter Hodgkiss, whose Ernest Press had originally agreed to publish the book.

Finally, grateful thanks to my family: to my daughter Emma for her sharp eye as a proof-reader, and to my wife Mary for her enduring support and encouragement.

Peter Berg,
Canterbury 2010

Introduction

Whymper the Lecturer

The name Edward Whymper is probably the one that comes most readily to mind when one thinks of British mountaineers of the 19th century: he was, after all, the leader of the group that first climbed the seemingly inaccessible Matterhorn, and the one who bore most blame for the tragic accident that occurred on the way down. Yet in many ways he was something of an outsider: he was not a gentleman of leisure, not an academic nor a lawyer with long periods of vacation, not an established artist or writer, but a talented wood engraver in an era before books and newspapers could use photographs as illustrations. His serious climbing career was relatively short, a few years in the Alps and one expedition to the Andes, and he wrote four books[1], apart from which his life was spent working in the family business. He was, though, accepted by the climbing community, was elected a member of the Alpine Club, and received considerable public support for his expedition to the Andes.

Chamonix guide book given to the Alpine Club, with the compliments of the author

It may be that the seeds of Whymper's fascination with the world of high mountains were sown in May 1858 when he was 18 years old and went to a lecture in London. He wrote in his diary afterwards:

In the evening I visited for the first time Mr Albert Smith's entertainment of Mont Blanc, etc… People often go to these sort of things with exorbitant expectations raised by previous descriptions which have been told them; I however found myself quite satisfied and more.[2]

Forty years later, in his Chamonix guidebook, Whymper wrote:

Mr. Albert Smith, a struggling literateur, conceived the idea that an ascent of Mont Blanc, illustrated by dioramic views, might be an exceedingly popular 'entertainment,' and he did not deceive himself. So popular did he make it that it would, doubtless, still be running if Albert Smith were still alive. Until his time the ascent of Mont Blanc was usually looked upon as a very serious business. Men commonly made their wills before starting for it, and wrote heavy accounts of the dangers of the enterprise when

---

[1] *Scrambles amongst the Alps in the years 1860-69*, Murray 1871; *Travels amongst the great Andes of the Equator*, Murray 1891-2; *Chamonix and the Range of Mont Blanc*, Murray 1896; *The Valley of Zermatt and the Matterhorn*, Murray 1897

[2] EW diary, 4 June 1858

they came down. Albert Smith invented a new treatment. In his hands the whole thing was a joke - a piece of sport. He made merry over his troubles, jested at the funny persons he met, and laughed at everything.

In 1851 he carried out his long-cherished desire, and attained the summit of Mont Blanc; and nine months afterwards produced at the Egyptian Hall, Piccadilly, an entertainment descriptive of the ascent, which 'took the world by storm, and became the most popular exhibition of the kind ever known.'

Whymper's own public speaking career dates back to the early 1860s. He was elected a member of the Alpine Club in December 1861, when he was only twenty-one, on the strength of the first ascent of Mont Pelvoux in the Dauphiné, and two years later he read a paper to the club on the subject of camping in the mountains. Then in September 1865, after the Matterhorn disaster, he gave a paper on the first ascent of the Aiguille Verte at a meeting of the British Association in Birmingham. His visit to Greenland in 1867 was the topic for several lectures in the early part of 1869. The 1879-80 expedition to the Andes provided the subject for lectures during the 1880s, including the occasion organized by the Alpine Club at the Royal Institution in 1881 before an audience of 900, at the end of which the Prince of Wales proposed a vote of thanks. After this, Whymper's lectures were largely about his alpine experiences, often in intensive campaigns of a few weeks, travelling all over the country: at the end of 1897, for example, he gave no fewer than twenty three lectures over a period of six weeks. In October 1900, he took his 'Scrambles' lecture to the United States, giving it ten times to audiences in New England whom he found unresponsive, but respectful. The last lecture about which we have any information was in Leeds in 1906.

Whymper took great pains to satisfy his audience. In the biography by Frank Smythe[3] it is reported that 'every word had to be written out and learnt; every phrase, nuance and gesture rehearsed again and again' and 'his clear forceful diction as well as his unfailing sense of the dramatic combined to make him and his lectures on the Alps and the Andes popular among audiences all over the country'.

---

[3] F S Smythe, Edward Whymper, Hodder and Stoughton 1940

In 1896, Whymper took a new lecture entitled 'My Scrambles Amongst the Alps' to Switzerland. It was given for the first time on August 10th in Davos:

'Began 10 minutes late, waiting for late arrivals. Took 1 hour and 25 minutes. The place was quite full and seats ran short. Bontwood the lantern man did pretty well, but he is slow with the double lantern, and his lenses are not good; the edges of the views were always out of focus. Was well received, but as the audience was two-thirds female, little applause and a good deal of whispering.' [4]

Whymper had a considerable talent for publicity, and in our day might have been a partner in a successful advertising agency. His two guidebooks, to the Zermatt area and to the Chamonix area, were very commercial, endpapers filled with advertisements for his own photographs and for products bearing his endorsement, and his lectures were clearly a means of promoting sales of books and pictures.

The Slides

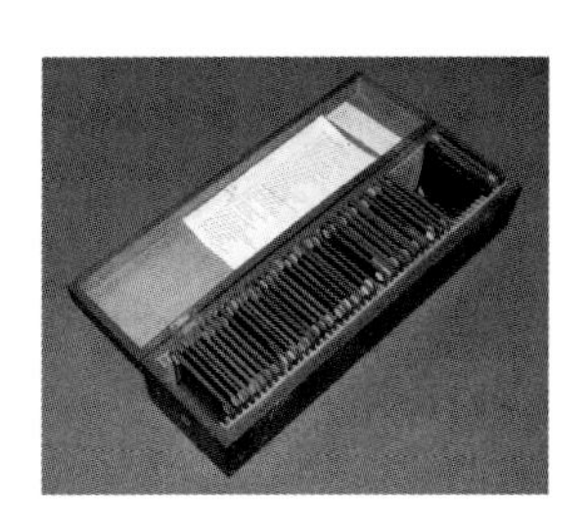

In the care of the Alpine Club are two boxes of magic lantern slides given to the Club in 1945. *The Alpine Journal* of the time[5] records the donation:

'Mrs M A Barron, of St Albans, has most kindly presented to the Club two boxes containing the identical lantern slides used by Edward Whymper for illustrating his lectures "My Scrambles Amongst the Alps". One box has the full complement of 50 slides, views in the Zermatt district, the other, 43 slides illustrating his climbs in the Mont Blanc district. All are most carefully indexed and in correct order. The Club offers its warm thanks to Mrs Barron for this most interesting gift.'

Extensive investigations have failed to reveal how Mrs Barron happened to have these slides. As far as we can tell, she was not related to Whymper,[6] and it is most likely that the slides were amongst his possessions sold by his brother after his death in 1912. Whatever their provenance, there seems little doubt that these are the illustrations for the 'Scrambles' lecture, and they may well be the set used that evening in Davos.

The lantern slides are contained in two fitted wooden boxes. Each has a neatly printed list of captions, together with emendations and comments

---

[4] EW diary, 10 August 1896

[5] Alpine Journal 55, 219, 1945-46

[6] EW's relatives Mrs Nigella Hall and the late Mr Timothy Woodgate knew of no relationship

for the operator in Whymper's own hand: 'Quick, vite' against certain groups, for example.

The slides are 3 ¼ inches square, double glass with passepartout edging, marked W. Watson & Sons, 313 High Holborn, London, Magic Lantern and Slide Manufacturers. Some are masked to give a circular or elliptical view.

Photography

Apart from three maps with hand-coloured sections, all are black-and-white or sepia, mostly taken from photographs. The subject matter of the photographs indicates that they were taken during visits to the Alps in 1893 - 1895 when Whymper was gathering material for his Chamonix and Zermatt guidebooks.

We know very little about the equipment that Whymper used for his photography, though there is a tantalizing reference to a camera in a letter from EW's nephew Robert to Frank Smythe, written in 1939:

'As a photographer EW was something of a pioneer, and he worked in conjunction, I believe, with the Ilford Company in perfecting the dry plate. I have seen some of his photos from the 'wet plate' era which were remarkably good. At any rate he was greatly interested in improving the dry plate, and at his death, I myself must have destroyed thousands of his experimental plates . His photograph taken of Queen Victoria's Jubilee from his office windows on Ludgate Hill is among his best later efforts. Incidentally I own one of EW's oldest and best cameras – consult A.B.Bradley of Peak, Frean, Bermondsey, London who is keeping it for me and using it continually.'

Dallmeyer field camera

All efforts to trace this camera have failed and it may well be that it was lost during the Second World War. It is likely that in the 1890s Whymper would have been using a whole-plate field camera. Cameras from Messrs. Ross and Messrs. Dallmeyer are advertised in the Chamonix guide, and Watsons of Holborn, who prepared the slides, also offered cameras, so he may well have been using equipment supplied by one of these firms.

Lantern-slide projectors were bulky pieces of equipment, often used in pairs or built as double projectors, as at the Davos lecture. Light sources would have been limelight, requiring oxygen and hydrogen cylinders, or incandescent electric lights. It is likely that these were provided by the

Newton lantern slide projector

organizers where Whymper was giving his lectures and could have been of a variety of different types and makes. Illustrated here is a projector like one owned by the Alpine Club, dating from just after the First World War, a 'Long Throw model D' manufactured by Newton & Co of Wigmore St. London.

Whymper's knowledge and experience of mountain photography is said to have been valuable to the Alpine Club in organising its collections of photographs and he showed his photographs of Equador at an AC exhibition.

The Lecture

Whymper opened his lecture with a slide showing a facsimile of the closing sentence of a letter from Lord Tennyson, the Poet Laureate. This tribute from one of the leading figures of the Victorian establishment clearly meant a good deal to Whymper. The accident that followed the first ascent of the Matterhorn in 1865 tinged Whymper's fame with notoriety, even after the success of his book *Scrambles amongst the Alps* published in 1871, but ten years later his successful expedition to the Andes was greeted with unreserved public approval.

Slides of two of Scheuchzer's dragons - which, presumably, Whymper did not find on any of his Alpine summits - and a general map of the western Alps are followed by thirty views of the villages and peaks of the Zermatt valley. It is interesting to note that while the villages appear simple and unspoiled, Zermatt itself a century ago was already highly developed with many substantial buildings. The slides include details of glacier features such as moulins, crevasses and séracs, as well as a charming group of children entitled 'Buy my edelweiss'.

The remainder of the first box consists of pictures from the Italian Ridge of the Matterhorn, probably a record of Whymper's visit in August 1895. There are no fewer than three pictures of 'Tumble Corner', below the Col du Lion, where he very nearly came to grief in 1862: no doubt the audience was treated to a graphic account of this event. The slide entitled 'Mutual Assistance', one climber on another's shoulders, probably raised a laugh, whilst a portrait of the guide Michel Croz, who lost his life in the 1865 accident, reminded listeners of the perils of mountaineering.

The second box takes us to Chamonix in July 1894, when Whymper made an ascent of Mont Blanc accompanied by the guides Daniel Maquignaz and Matthias Zurbriggen, with a young man called Paul Breton to carry the photographic equipment. He was incensed by the roster system of allocating guides at Chamonix, and may have commented on the slide of the 'Bureau des Guides' with sarcastic words from his diary of the previous year:

Visited Guide Chief to ask his permission to allow me a guide and five porters for Mont Blanc. He graciously allowed me.

On this occasion the party spent two nights at the Janssen Observatory on the summit of the mountain. A picture shows a snowy interior, and with the temperature inside falling as low as 19°F, it can hardly have been a comfortable experience. Whymper clearly had his tongue in his cheek when he placed slides of Dr Janssen next to another of a dragon and then one of the learned doctor himself being carried up the mountain in a litter. And we have guides falling into crevasses and breaking though snow bridges in very contrived photographs which provoke a smile these days, even if they were intended to strike terror into the hearts of audiences a hundred years ago. The series finishes with portraits of Frédéric Payot, one of Whymper's last visitors before he died in Chamonix in September 1911, and two of Melchior Anderegg, the 'Melchior' whose name in Switzerland, according to *Scrambles*, was as well known as that of Napoleon. So ended Whymper's lecture, with a tribute to one of the men who made the Golden Age of mountaineering possible.

This is a remarkable collection of photographs, even if it does not capture the most dramatic moments of mountaineering expeditions - hardly possible with the cameras of the period - and dates from long after Whymper's principal achievements in the field. Quite apart from the technical and artistic quality of many of the slides - the picture of the Boden Glacier, for example - they show what it was that Whymper believed to be significant and of interest to the public, as well as giving us a little insight into his character and sense of humour.

Reconstruction

Most of the text in this reconstruction of the lecture 'My Scrambles in the Alps' is taken from Whymper's own writings, published and unpublished. Where further text has been necessary I have used extracts from books by his contemporaries such as Forbes, Tyndall, Smith and Coolidge, as well as more recent writers including R.L.G. Irving, Guido Rey and EW's biographer, Frank Smythe. These are all identified where they appear. Where there is no attribution, the comments are mine. The text is further embellished with engravings and wood-cuts from Whymper's books. Details of all the sources are given at the end of this book.

Whymper's spellings of proper names are variable:
I have used slide titles and texts as he wrote them, adding clarification where necessary.

His texts and those of his contemporaries are in Roman type; my comments are in Italics. I've also taken the liberty of altering the sequence of slides in some cases with the aim of improving continuity and presentation.

My Scrambles Amongst the Alps

A magic lantern lecture by Edward Whymper

R. S. J. Macdonald

In the year 1860, shortly before leaving England for a long continental tour, a certain eminent London publisher requested me to make for him some sketches of the great alpine peaks. At this time I had only a literary acquaintance with mountaineering, and had even not seen – much less set foot upon – a mountain. Amongst the peaks which were upon my list was Mont Pelvoux, in Dauphiné. The sketches required of it were to celebrate the triumph of some Englishmen who intended make its ascent. They came – they saw – but they did not conquer. By a mere chance I fell in with a very agreeable Frenchman who accompanied this party, and was pressed by him to return to the assault. In 1861 we did so, with my friend Macdonald – and we conquered. This was the origin of my scrambles amongst the Alps.

Mount Pelvoux in the Dauphine

The ascent of Mont Pelvoux was a very delightful scramble. The mountain air did not act as an emetic; the sky did not look black, instead of blue; nor did I feel tempted to throw myself over precipices. I hastened to enlarge my experience, to the Matterhorn. I was urged to Mont Pelvoux by those mysterious impulses which cause men to peer into the unknown. Not only was this the mountain reputed to be the highest in France and on that account was worthy of attention, but it was the dominating point of a most picturesque district of the highest interest, which, to this day [1870], remains almost unexplored! The Matterhorn attracted me simply by its grandeur. It was considered to be the most thoroughly inaccessible of all mountains, even by those who ought to have known better. Stimulated to make fresh exertions by one repulse after another, I returned, year after year, as I had the opportunity, more and more determined to find a way up it, or to prove it to be really inaccessible.

This was the start of a most remarkable six years of alpine enterprise, achieving first ascent after first ascent, culminating with the Matterhorn in 1865 and its tragic aftermath.

It is a matter for speculation why EW chose to begin a lecture entitled 'My Scrambles in the Alps' with this particular letter of thanks from the late Poet Laureate. It not thought likely that Tennyson had been present at the lecture EW gave about the Andes expedition at the Royal Institution in 1881, after which the Prince of Wales proposed a vote of thanks, but, from the full text of the letter, we know that EW sent Tennyson a copy of Travels Amongst the Great Andes of the Equator *published ten years later. We also know that the Whympers and the Tennysons had been neighbours in Haslemere, Surrey, for many years. EW's father Josiah took Town House in the village in 1859 and lived there until his death in 1903, and it is said EW did most of his later writing in the study there.*

I don't think that I have ever
been higher than about 7000
feet, & so I look up to you
Chimborazoan & Cotopaxian
with all the greater veneration

Yours very truly
Tennyson

Slide 01: LETTER FROM TENNYSON

The manuscript of this letter, one of the last Tennyson wrote, is at Yale. The body of the letter is in a different hand, probably that of his son Hallam, with the somewhat shaky signature added by the poet himself.

Alfred, Lord Tennyson

The Town House in the Surrey village of Haselmere.

Lord Tennyson built a grand house in the nearby hamlet of Aldworth, using it as his main residence from 1867 for the remaining twenty-five years of his life. Tennyson's death in October 1892 would have been a recent event for EW's audience in 1896 and these words of praise from one of the greatest figures of the age would have had considerable impact.

One of the principal aims of the 1879/80 Andes expedition was to investigate the effect of high altitude on the human body.

Evidence is overwhelming that, from 14,000 feet above the level of the sea and upwards, serious inconveniences have frequently occurred; that prostration (amounting in the more extreme cases to incapacitation) has been experienced; and that in a few instances, perhaps, even death has resulted through some cause which operates at great elevations. The evidence has come from all parts of the world, and has accumulated during several centuries. It has been afforded, independently, by multitudes of persons of diverse conditions – by cultured men of science down to illiterate peasants, the latter of whom cannot have heard of experiences beyond their own; and, although the testimony often differs in detail it agrees in the general leading features. Nausea and vomiting; headaches of severe character; feverishness; haemorrhages; lassitude, depression and weakness, and an indescribable feeling of illness, have been repeatedly mentioned as occurring at great elevations, and have only been cured by descending into lower zones. To these maladies the term Mountain Sickness is now commonly applied. This subject, long since, appeared to me to be worthy of investigation for its own sake, more particularly for ascertaining the height at which effects begin to manifest themselves; the symptoms; and whether the effects are permanent.

EW's original plan was to go to the Himalayas but when this area was placed out of bounds by the British authorities, he turned to South America. Hostilities between Chile, Peru and Bolivia ruled out the highest parts of the Andes, leaving Ecuador as the only remaining suitable country. This expedition, fully supported by the governments of Britain and Ecuador as well as by the Alpine Club, achieved ascents of Chimborazo (20,498ft/6247m), Cotopaxi (19,613ft/5978m) and other mountains, and assembled a variety of useful scientific information. EW's companions on the trip were his old guide and rival, Jean-Antoine Carrel, with a cousin, Louis Carrel, both from the Aosta valley.

Even in EW's days the high mountains were widely believed to be inhabited by terrifying beasts. Of the Matterhorn he writes:

There seemed to be a cordon drawn around it, up to which one might go, but no farther. Within that invisible line gins and effreets were supposed to exist – the Wandering Jew and the spirits of the damned. The superstitious natives in the surrounding valleys spoke of a ruined city on its summit wherein the spirits dwelt; and if you laughed, they gravely shook their heads; told you to look yourself to see the castles and walls, and warned one against a rash approach, lest the infuriate demons from their impregnable heights might hurl down vengeance for one's derision. Such were the traditions of the natives.

The Swiss scholar Johann Jakob Scheuchzer published in 1723 an account of his journeys in the mountains, including reports by men of good faith who had seen dragons in Switzerland. He himself doubted their existence, though he illustrates the reports with fanciful representations of the animals as seen here.

But as R.L.G.Irving wrote 'A beast whose slaughter would have secured immortality for the lucky sportsman and headlines for a week in every European newspaper is the dragon. Unfortunately the genus draco disappeared in the eighteenth century, or rather was exterminated by scepticism'

Slide 02: A FLYING DRAGON

Slide 03: ANOTHER DRAGON

The first trip, in 1860, took EW through the Bernese Oberland, over the Gemmi pass to the Rhone valley, to Zermatt and surrounding valleys, to Martigny and the Great St Bernard pass, up the Valpelline and over the mountains to Breuil (now better known as Cervinia), to Courmayeur and Chamonix, to Turin, past Monte Viso to the Dauphiné and a close view of Mont Pelvoux, finishing with a 70 mile walk from Briançon to Grenoble in steady rain in 18 hours actual walking time!

In 1861 EW returned to the Dauphiné, climbing Monte Pelvoux and making an attempt on Monte Viso over the border in Italy before continuing to Breuil and making his first attempt on the Matterhorn.

1862 saw four further failed attempts on the Matterhorn, followed in 1863 by success on the Grand Tournalin and another Matterhorn failure. In 1864 EW made a number of first ascents in the Écrins and the Mont Blanc massif, but further efforts on the Matterhorn had to be postponed for business reasons.

The 1865 season was the most remarkable of all, with ascents of the Grand Cornier, the Grandes Jorasses, the Aiguille Verte and finally the Matterhorn itself.

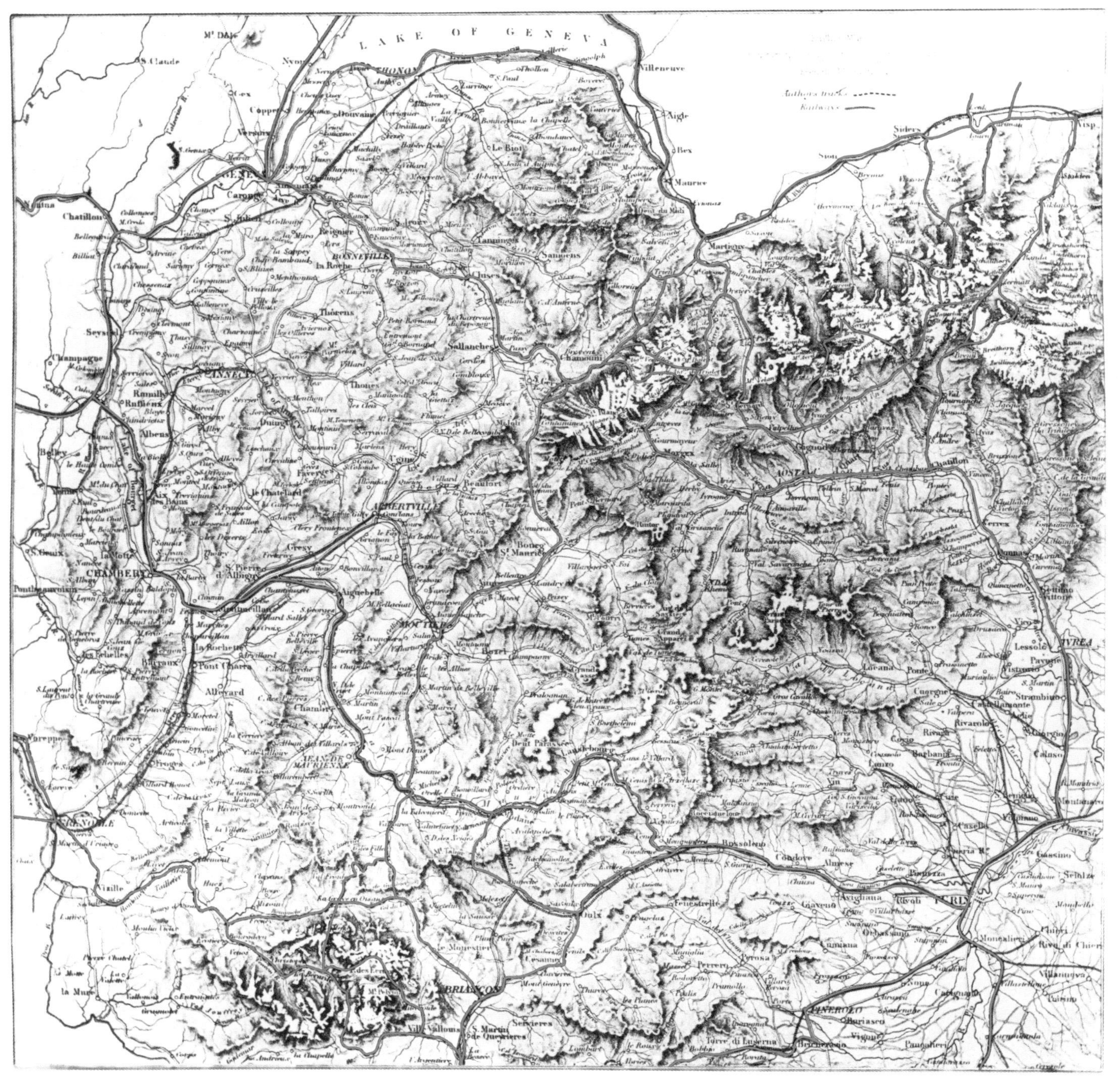

Slide 04: MAP OF THE WESTERN ALPS.
EW's travels in the 1860s are marked on the map with green lines.

Whymper, always punctilious in planning his journeys and a great fount of information for the traveller, no doubt wished to pass some of this on to his audience.

The most direct way to Zermatt either from London or Paris is by the Paris, Lyons and Mediterranean Railway via Dijon, Pontarlier, Vallorbe and Lausanne. The best train for those who wish to travel straight through is the night express, which leaves the Gare de Lyon at or about 9.10 p.m. If this is taken, you should be landed at Zermatt in the following afternoon, in time to settle down before dinner.

After Lausanne, the railway goes up the Rhône Valley, and in due course arrives at the entrance of the valley leading to Zermatt.

Get your things together, for in a few minutes you will be at Visp (buffet, good) where, as there is a break of gauge, *all for Zermatt must change.*

Visp is picturesquely situated on the left bank of the Rhône at the entrance to the Visp Thal. Five miles to the south this valley divides – the western branch (the Valley of St Nicholas or Nicolai Thal) leading to Zermatt, and the eastern one (Valley of Saas or Saas Thal) to the villages of Saas and Saas-Fée, and to the Monte Moro Pass.

Slide 05: VISP

At Visp the one metre gauge rack railway from Brig leaves the Rhône Valley to ascend the Vispertal on the climb up to Zermatt.

The station of the Zermatt Railway is alongside of that of the Jura-Simplon Railway. The line is 35 kilometres in length, and the difference in level between Visp and Zermatt, 3,200 feet, might have been overcome by a ruling gradient of 1 in 36. If anything like this had been employed, very heavy and costly works would have been necessary; but they have been avoided by adopting the 'système Abt'.

Mountain climber locomotive 1898

Where the ground is flat, the line skims the surface, and where there is an abrupt rise in the floor of the valley there are steep gradients upon which a third, rack rail (crémaillère) is laid. The line presents therefore a succession of moderate inclines and very rapid ones. In some places the railway rises as much as one foot in eight. The third rail is not used when the gradients are less than one in forty, and is laid over only five miles.

It is composed of two plates of steel which are bolted together in such a manner that the teeth alternate. The engines have two mechanisms – one for the ordinary rails and the other for the crémaillère. It is said that there are never less than four teeth biting at a time. In ascending the steep inclines the pace drops to four miles an hour and less. Great caution is used in descending; and, on the sections with the crémaillère, the trains

Slide 05A: THE SYSTEME ABT COG RAIL

seldom travel so fast as three miles an hour. There are several guardians to watch the line, who inspect the whole of it between the passage of each train. The early trains, during the season, are generally overfilled with passengers, eager to see the view.

This beautiful old bridge stands close by the Neubrücke halt.

There are a remarkable number of points of view in the Valley, some of which are only seen from the path, and others from the railway. A tourist who wishes to obtain a comprehensive idea of the valley should go one way by the path.

For the first 5 kilometres from Visp the road and railway keep close together, but at Neubrücke the path crosses to the left bank of the stream by a bold single-arch bridge.

The mountains seen in front when coming up this part of the valley are at the northern end of the Saas Grat or range of the Mischabelhörner, separating the Nicolai Thal from the Saas Thal.

Slide 06: NEUBRUCKE

Stalden is the small village where the already narrow valley forks, the eastern arm leading up to Saas Fee, the Zermatt railway following the western arm.

Stalden is 7 ½ km from Visp. A good deal of Muscat wine is made in the neighbourhood. It used to be procurable at 70 to 80 centimes a bottle. Prices have risen.

'I had an opportunity at Stalden,' said Forbes, 'of witnessing here a remarkable scene. A comedy was to be acted by peasants dressed in costume, who were to perform on a stage erected in the open air. There were not less than forty actors, the female parts being performed by men, and the costumes were elaborately and ingeniously devised. The piece named "Rosa of Tannenburg" was preluded by a procession of the actors, amongst the most conspicuous of whom were three devils attired in tight suits of black, with horns and tails, the senior wearing goat's horns and the subordinates those of the chamois'.

Principal James G Forbes

'The entertainment was under the patronage, and even direction of the clergy, and one of the curates seemed to be master of ceremonies, for he was frequently seen in earnest conversation with the junior devil with the chamois horns. I must add, that the scene was one of the most romantic which can be conceived. Behind the village was a truly natural theatre, with a green meadow for the pit, while a range of low cliffs, with a concave front festooned with ivy and brushwood, represented the boxes and gallery.'

Slide 07: STALDEN

This picture, looking southwards up the long Vispertal, appears to have been taken near Kalpetran between Stalden and St Nicholas. It is characteristic of the valley with its fertile floor beneath bold, truncated spurs with always a glimpse of the snows far above.

The Leslie Stephen quote comes from his article in the Alpine Journal Vol I (p.43) on the second ascent of the Weisshorn.

The summit of the Weisshorn can be seen behind the Brunegghorn from Stalden nearly up to Kalpetran. The Weisshorn, 14,803 feet, is not so happily placed as the Matterhorn and other peaks which might be mentioned, and it cannot anywhere be seen to advantage from a low level. But from moderate and from the higher elevations it always appears a grand mountain. 'Of all the mountain tops I know,' wrote Leslie Stephen 'that of the Weisshorn is, I think, the most beautiful, with perhaps the one exception of the Wetterhorn. It is formed by three of those firm and delicate edges which can only be modeled in the mountain snow, uniting to meet in a mathematical point.' The first ascent was made on Aug. 18-19, 1861, by the guides J.J.Bennen and Ulrich Wenger (an Oberlander) with Dr.John Tyndall.

Leslie Stephen

J. J. Bennen

Dr. John Tyndall

Slide 08: UP ZERMATT VALLEY

As it emerged from a short tunnel a short distance above Stalden, the Zermatt railway spanned the Mühlebach torrent on this 67 metre (220 ft) bridge built in 1890. It was replaced with a concrete arch in 1959.

The large bridge over the Mühlebach is passed just before km 9, and shortly afterwards the path for a kilometre and a half is of a superior order, and is carried along a shelf cut out of the slopes, nearly at a level.

The Mattervisp torrent, at this part, runs through a deep gorge or defile, which is better seen from the railway than from the path.

Kalpetran is only a small group of chalets, no inn.

Store House

Slide 09: KALPETRAN BRIDGE

The ancient, onion-domed church stands opposite the railway station of St Niklaus (St Nicholas), once the capital of the valley. Here was the birthplace of famous guides, including the Lochmatter family (from 1825) and the great Joseph Knubel (1881-1961).

The village of St Nicholas was much damaged by the earthquake of 1855 and was not thoroughly restored several years afterwards. The Church suffered considerably. This edifice has also been twice nearly destroyed by avalanches from the Sparrhorn which descend through a ravine on the west of the village. An avalanche in 1618 wrecked the tower and choir, and another in 1750 destroyed the remainder.

Lord Minto, when at St Nicholas in 1830, was struck by the cheese that was set before him by the Curé. 'I had coveted,' he said, 'the remains of a delightful piece of old cheese upon which we had feasted...and he presented it to me... The prize which I carried off was about twenty years old, perfectly fresh and pungent, like a fine old ewes-milk cheese in Scotland...We had one cheese put before us which we were told was thirty years old; it was perfectly fresh and good.'

Anyone who expects to stand a long siege should buy it, for it is said that it will keep for fifty years!

Slide 10: ST NICHOLAS

Whymper seems to have found beggars and roadside sellers of flowers and fruit troublesome, none more so than on one occasion on the road up to the Col de la Forclaz from Martigny.

The path from Martigny to the summit has undergone successive improvements in these latter years; but mendicants permanently disfigure it.

We passed many tired pedestrians toiling up this oven, persecuted by trains of parasitic children. These children swarm like maggots in a rotten cheese. They carry baskets of fruit with which to plague the weary tourist. They flit around him like flies; they thrust the fruit in his face; they pester him with their pertinacity. Beware of them! - taste, touch not their fruit.

Slide 11: BUY MY EDELWEIS

The small village of Täsch is a convenient starting place for climbing the Weisshorn and the Mischabel peaks. It also now marks the end of the public road up the valley.

In the village of Täsch there is little to be seen except the collection of skulls and bones which is preserved in a small building attached to the church. At Täsch and various other places, they do not allow one to remain peaceably in his grave in perpetuity. You are disinterred and your bones are stacked away in this fashion.

Slide 12: BONES AT TASCH

Zermatt, at some 1600m/5,250 ft, has hugely expanded since this picture was taken. It looks south-west towards the foot of the Matterhorn from the slopes above the modern suburb of Ried. The terminus of the Gornergrat cog railway now occupies the one-time meadows in the centre of the picture, while the tunnel of the Sunnegga funicular rises from the modern suburb of Weisti at the bottom left.

The village of Zermatt is situated in a basin at the head of the Nicolai Thal, upon nearly level ground, on the left bank of the Mattervisp torrent.

The permanent population at the last Census was 525, and it is now estimated at 600. During the season, the residents are largely augmented by the persons employed in the Hotels, and by shopkeepers and others who come from various parts of Switzerland.

The whole of the upper parts of the surrounding Alps and mountains, up to the limits of pasturage, are the property of the Commune. On the lower ground, many little patches and plots are private property. The Zermatters set a high value on their land, and ask prices equivalent to those which are obtainable in the City of London.

Until 1852, the only hotel at Zermatt was a little inn kept by the village doctor, Lauber, which was started in 1839. In 1854, the Lauber inn was acquired by Mons. Alexandre Seiler, who christened it Hotel du Mont Rose. M. Seiler understood the art of inn-keeping. He knew how to welcome the coming and to speed the parting guest, and soon made a name for the Mont Rose. If anyone enquired 'What is the best hotel in Zermatt?' or 'Where should we go?' the answer was 'Go to the Monte Rosa' or 'Go to Seiler's.'

Nearly simultaneously with the foundation of the latter hotel, the outburst of British energy occurred which led to the subjugation of all the High Alps around Zermatt.

Following the foundation of the Alpine Club in 1857, the Monte Rosa came to be known as 'The Club-Room of Zermatt'

The Club-Room of Zermatt 1864

Slide 13: ZERMATT

This classic shot of the Matterhorn (4478m/14,690ft) is taken from almost the same viewpoint as the previous picture of Zermatt. It shows the precipitous North Face bounded by the Zmutt (N.W.) Ridge on the right and the Hörnli (N.E.) Ridge on the left. The East Face is shrouded in cloud.

It is unnecessary to enter into a minute description of the Matterhorn, after all that has been written about that famous mountain. Those by whom this book is likely to be read will know that that peak is nearly 15,000 feet high, and that it rises abruptly, by a series of cliffs which may properly be termed precipices, a clear 5,000 feet above the glaciers which surround its base. They will know too that it was the last great Alpine peak which remained unscaled, less on account of the difficulty of doing so, than from the terror inspired by its invincible appearance.

Slide 14: THE MATTERHORN IN CLOUD

This slide is the first of a series showing the main peaks in the vicinity of the Matterhorn.

The Dent Blanche (4357m/14,293ft) is seen from the south-east with the long South Ridge, climbed in 1862, on the left and the Arête des Quatre Anes (E.N.E. Ridge or Viereselgrat), first climbed in 1882, on the right. The Pointe de Zinal is the small peak in the mid-distance.

Earlier in 1862 Thomas Kennedy had made an attempt at a winter ascent of the Hörnli Ridge of the Matterhorn, though his party did not get very far, beaten back by strong winds.

The first ascent of the Dent Blanche was made on July 18 1862, by Mr T. S. Kennedy and Mr W. Wigram, with the guides Jean-Baptiste Croz (brother of Michel-Auguste) and J Kronig of Zermatt, under unfavourable conditions. They started from the chalets of Abricolla on the eastern side of the Glacier de Ferpecle, about 3 hours from Evolena, and ascended partly by the SW face, and partly by the ridge running southwards from the summit, taking 16 hours from Abricolla and back.

T. S. Kennedy

Slide 15: DENT BLANCHE

With its formidable North Face rising over the Grenz Glacier, a tributary of the great Gorner Glacier, and its crest a full 2 kilometers / 1 ¼ miles in length, the Lyskamm (4527m/14,852ft) was first climbed in 1861. The Lysjoch (4151m/13,619ft) is the snowy saddle on the far left. The Monte Rosa or Bétemps Hut (newly built in 1895) can just be discerned in the Plattje rocks at the bottom left in this view southwards from the Gornergrat.

The Lyskamm is exceeded in elevation by mountains in the Zermatt district only by Monte Rosa and the Dom. The first ascent was made in 1861.

The col between the Lyskamm and Ludvigshohe is called the Lysjoch. In 1894, a dramatic incident occurred on the Zermatt side of the Lysjoch. Her Majesty the Queen of Italy was crossing the pass on Aug. 25, with a caravan of 30 persons, led by Alessandro Welf of Gressoney, under the general direction of Baron Louis Peccoz. The summit was crossed, and for the first hour-and-a-half Her Majesty and two ladies were dragged down in sledges. When this manner of progression could no longer be continued, Welf took the lead, followed by the Baron and the Queen. Presently they approached some crevasses, and the Baron called out loudly 'Crevasses! Take care of the Queen!' A few seconds afterwards, Welf felt a pull on the rope, and, turning, saw the Baron falling on the snow. The others gathered around, but they could do nothing. Baron Peccoz gave one or two gasps, and expired.

Slide 16: LYSKAMM

This picture fits exactly onto the right hand margin of the previous picture, Slide 16. Here the 'Twins' rise between the Lyskamm, out of the picture on the left, and the Roccia Nera (4075m/13,369ft) – the South East Buttress of the Breithorn – on the right. The Zwillings Glacier falls below Castor (4228m/13,971ft) on the left and the Schwarze Glacier from Pollux (4092m/13,425ft) on the right, to join the Gorner Glacier at the bottom of the picture.

Castor and Pollux (Zwillinge or the Twins) are overshadowed by the Lyskamm and the Breithorn. They can both be bagged in one day from the Zwillingepass.

Castor, 13,878 feet, 4230 metres, was ascended by Messrs. W. Mathews and F. W. Jacomb with Michel-Auguste Croz and J. B. Croz, on Aug. 23, 1861, in 1 hr. from the Zwillingepass; and Pollux, 13,422 feet, 4094 metres, is said to have been first ascended by Mons. Jules Jacot in 1864, from the Schwarztor.

Slide 17: TWINS

Seen to the north-west from near Schwarzsee, this view shows the ice-hung North Face of the Breithorn (now reckoned to be 4164m/13,661ft) on which there are several fine routes, the earliest dating back to 1869. Like the nearby Twins and Lyskamm, the Breithorn is a frontier peak and is usually climbed on foot or on ski via the easy-angled southern, Italian flank.

In 1792, after measuring the height of the Matterhorn, De Saussure and his son went up the Petit Mont Cervin [Klein Matterhorn] and said that at that time it had never been ascended by mortal man. The De Saussures declined the ascent of the Breithorn, partly on account of 'the fatigue and dangers which the steepness of the slopes would have caused them 'and also because examination of its rocks could not be made, from their being entirely covered with snow 'As it,' he said, 'presents a large and rounded summit to those who approach it on the side of Zermatt, the name Breit-Horn or Cime-Large appears to suit it very well.'

The Breithorn is said to have been first ascended by Mons. Henri Maynard in 1813. Lord Minto went up the Breithorn in 1830, with his son William (a boy of sixteen), who 'excited much compassion [at Zermatt] as they thought it hard that so young a boy should be led up to perish so cruelly.'

The ascent of the Breithorn 13,685 feet, 4171 metres, has become extremely popular. The panorama that may be enjoyed from the top is one of the finest (some say the finest) that can be seen in the Zermatt district; and, although less extensive, is more picturesque than the views from the summits of the still loftier peaks.

Slide 18: BREITHORN

This interesting picture - originally captioned by EW, wrongly, as the Findeln Glacier - looks south-east towards the Breithorn from the chalets of Hermettje (2053m/6,735ft) on the Schwarzsee path. The glacier is the Gornergletscher, one of the longest in the Alps, but its snout, known as the Bodengletscher and seen here at the bottom of the picture, has now retreated to the foot of the conspicuous big black buttress of the Lichenbretter some 2km/1 ¼ miles back.

The excursion by the Fluh Alp to the Findelen Glacier, and round by the Stockhorn Pass, returning down the whole length of the Gorner Glacier, is the finest of its description that can be made from Zermatt. Every phase in the life of a glacier, from its cradle to its grave, can be seen upon it. There are crevasses, open and concealed; seracs and ice-falls; glacier rivers and moulins; glacier tables and moraines.

Slide 19: BODEN GLACIER

This picture, and the three that follow, which could well illustrate characteristic features on the dry section of any alpine glacier, were shot on the Mer de Glace between Montenvers and its junction with the tributary Leschaux and Talèfre Glaciers – as is evidenced by the distant glimpse of the Grands Jorasses in Slide 20. In the junction area especially, many surface streams still plunge into profound and frightening-looking moulins. In Victorian times Montenvers, with its rustic hotel, was a favourite and safe location for visitors to 'sample' a real glacier, and with the opening of the rack railway in 1908 it became a tourist mecca.

In this picture EW shows his party crossing a highly-crevassed section of a glacier. Professor Forbes describes glacier travel like this:

Urged onwards in its flow upon the immense bed of rocks on which it reposes, forced sometimes to discharge itself over the bank of a precipice, the rigid mass is fissured in all directions. Swayed hither and thither by the unevenness of its base, the fissures maintain no constant direction, but subdivide the ponderous mass into rude, prismatic fragments, whose height is the thickness of the ice, and the form of their bases is determined by the meeting of the fissures which form them... To make much way along such glaciers as these is, evidently, next to impossible. The experienced guide will either cross the glacier as directly as possible, if his course requires him to do so, or scale the rocky walls of the ravine in preference to attempting to follow the course of the glacier. Such excursions, even when not dangerous, are the most fatiguing of all sorts of climbing – the traveller now leaping from point to point along the jagged edges of the ice which bound the fissures; now making long zig-zags to get round the crevasses which cannot possibly be traversed; at other times descending the walls of those less steep and profound, and laboriously climbing the opposite face.

Slide 20: AMONG THE CREVASSES

In June 1865 EW went up the Mer de Glace and the Talèfre Glacier on his way to the Aiguille Verte.

On a proof print of this photograph EW noted: a few sparkles might be put on the water. This done to shew a glacier stream.

Our course led us over the old Mer de Glace – the glacier made famous by De Saussure and Forbes. The heat of the day was over, but the little rills and rivulets were still flowing along the surface of the ice; cutting deep troughs where the gradients were small; leaving ripple-marks where the water was with more difficulty confined to one channel; and falling over the precipitous walls of the great crevasses, sometimes in bounding cascades, and sometimes in diffused streams, which marked the perpendicular faces with graceful sinuosities. As night came on, their music died away, the rivulets dwindled down to rills; the rills ceased to murmur, and the sparkling drops, caught by the hand of frost, were bound to the ice, coating it with an enamelled film which lasted until the sun struck the glacier once more.

Slide 21: GLACIER STREAM

On the proof of this picture EW wrote:
distant figure to be touched out, gleam of light at top of water...

Coolidge:

Stones lie on the surface of the ice, so the little streams that run over the surface in the daytime cannot pursue a straight course perpendicular to the glacier, but are forced to hollow out crooked channels for themselves. Now when a stream of this kind meets with a hole in the ice, still more when the hole is large enough to be dignified by the name of a crevasse, the water naturally seeks an issue towards the rock-bed beneath the glacier. The falling water little by little wears away the ice and enlarges this hole, so that a vertical shaft is formed down which the stream rushes in a waterfall. The waterfalls so formed are called *moulins* or *Glacier Mills.*

Slide 22: MOULIN

Coolidge:

The surface of a glacier is not smooth and level, like a skating rink. It rises, even where roughly level, in many humps or hummocks, caused in general by the varying action of the sun's rays on the surface according as it is protected by sand or stones, or not protected. Sometimes these humps are cones of some feet in height, and are capped by a great boulder, which has intercepted the action of the sun's rays; these ice pillars, crowned by a great rock, are known as Glacier Tables, and are among the most striking of glacial phenomena.

Slide 23: GLACIER TABLE

At times, crevasses can take the form of caverns, in this case where an underground glacier stream pours out at the foot of a glacier. This picture may well show the snout of the Mer de Glace, the source of the Aveyron torrent, a major tributary of the Arve. In 1896 the ice extended to about 170 m/560ft above the flat valley floor, but today it has retreated 200 m/650ft higher up and over a kilometre along the ground.

Tyndall:

The Gorner Glacier, as we ascend it towards the old Weissthor, presents many fine examples of such crevasses; the ice being often torn in a most curious and irregular manner. You enter a porch, pillared by icicles, and look into a cavern in the very body of the glacier, encumbered with vast frozen bosses which are fringed all round by dependent icicles. At the peril of your life from slipping, or from the yielding of the stalactites, you may enter these caverns, and find yourself steeped in the blue illumination of the place. Their beauty is beyond description; but you cannot deliver yourself up, heart and soul, to its enjoyment. There is a strangeness about the place which repels you, and not without anxiety do you look from your ledge into the darkness below, through which the sound of subglacial water sometimes rises like the tolling of distant bells. You feel that, however, the cold splendours of the place might suit a purely spiritual essence, they are not congenial to flesh and blood, and you gladly escape from its magnificence to the sunshine of the world above.

Slide 24: GLACIER CAVERN

The beautiful North Face of the Obergabelhorn is a tapering sweep of steep ice which breaks into this ice fall towards its foot as the angle eases. It then merges into several other ice streams to become the extensive Glacier de Zinal. This view across the foot of the Face looks south-west from the Triftjoch (3527m/11,572ft).

Tyndall describes what happens when a glacier moves over a steep drop in its bed:

Over this summit the glacier is pushed, and has its back periodically broken, thus forming vast transverse ridges which follow each other in succession down the slope. At the summit these ridges are often cleft by fissures transverse to them, thus forming detached towers of ice of the most picturesque and imposing character. These towers often fall; and while some are caught on the platforms of the cascade, others struggle with the slow energy of a behemoth through the debris which opposes them, reach the edges of the precipices which rise in succession along the fall, leap over, and, amid ice-smoke and thunder-peals, fight their way downwards.

To such towers the name Séracs is applied. In the chalets of Savoy, after the richer curd has been precipitated by rennet, a stronger acid is used to throw down what remains; an inferior kind of cheese call Sérac is thus formed, the shape and colour of which have suggested the application of the term to the cubical masses of ice.

Slide 25: SERACS ON GABELHORN

The rocky outcrop called the Lychenbretter (Lichenbretter) lies between the Théodule and Gorner Glaciers. Even in EW's day the glaciers had retreated some way from their extent during the so-called Little Ice Age of the mid 17th. century. Once the ice has shrunk, abandoned rock faces and moraine slopes remain loose, unstable and chaotic for many years. Today these unpleasant-looking cliffs rear over the very snout of the Gorner Glacier.

This area presented EW with serious difficulties during his first visit to Zermatt in 1860.

At Zermatt I wandered in many directions, but the weather was bad, and my work was much retarded. One day, after spending a long time in attempts to sketch near the Hornli, and in futile endeavours to seize the forms of the peaks as they for a few seconds peered out from above the dense banks of woolly clouds, I determined not to return to Zermatt by the usual path, but to cross the Gorner glacier to the Riffel hotel. After a rapid scramble over the polished rocks and snowbeds which skirt the base of the Theodule glacier, and wading through some of the streams which flow from it, at that time much swollen by the late rains, the first difficulty was arrived at, in the shape of a precipice about three hundred feet high. It seemed there would be no difficulty in crossing the glacier if the cliff could be descended. The general contour of the cliff was nearly perpendicular, but it was a good deal broken up, and there was little difficulty in descending by zigzagging from one mass to another.

At length EW found himself down by the ice:

At this moment a second difficulty presented itself. The glacier swept round an angle of cliff, and as the ice was not of the nature of treacle or thin putty, it kept away from the little bay on which I stood. All along the side of the cliff, as far as could be seen in both directions, the ice did not touch it, but there was this marginal crevasse, seven feet wide, and of unknown depth.

All this could be seen at a glance, and almost at once I concluded that I could not jump the crevasse, and began to try along the cliff lower down; but without success, for the ice rose higher and higher, until at last further progress was stopped by the cliffs becoming perfectly smooth. With an axe it would have been possible to cut up the side of the ice; without one I saw there was no alternative but to return and face the jump.

It was getting towards evening, and the solemn stillness of the High Alps was broken only by the sound of rushing water or of falling rocks. If the jump should be successful – well; if not, I fell into that horrible chasm, to be frozen in, or drowned in that gurgling, rushing water. Everything depended on that jump. Again I asked myself, 'Can it be done?' It *must* be. So, finding my stick was useless, I threw it and the sketch-book to the ice, and first retreating as far as possible, ran forward with all my might, took the leap, barely reached the other side, and fell awkwardly on my knees. Almost at the same moment a shower of stones fell on the spot from which I had jumped.

Slide 26: THE LYCHENBRETTER

Slide 27: THE LYCHENBRETTER, *closer view*

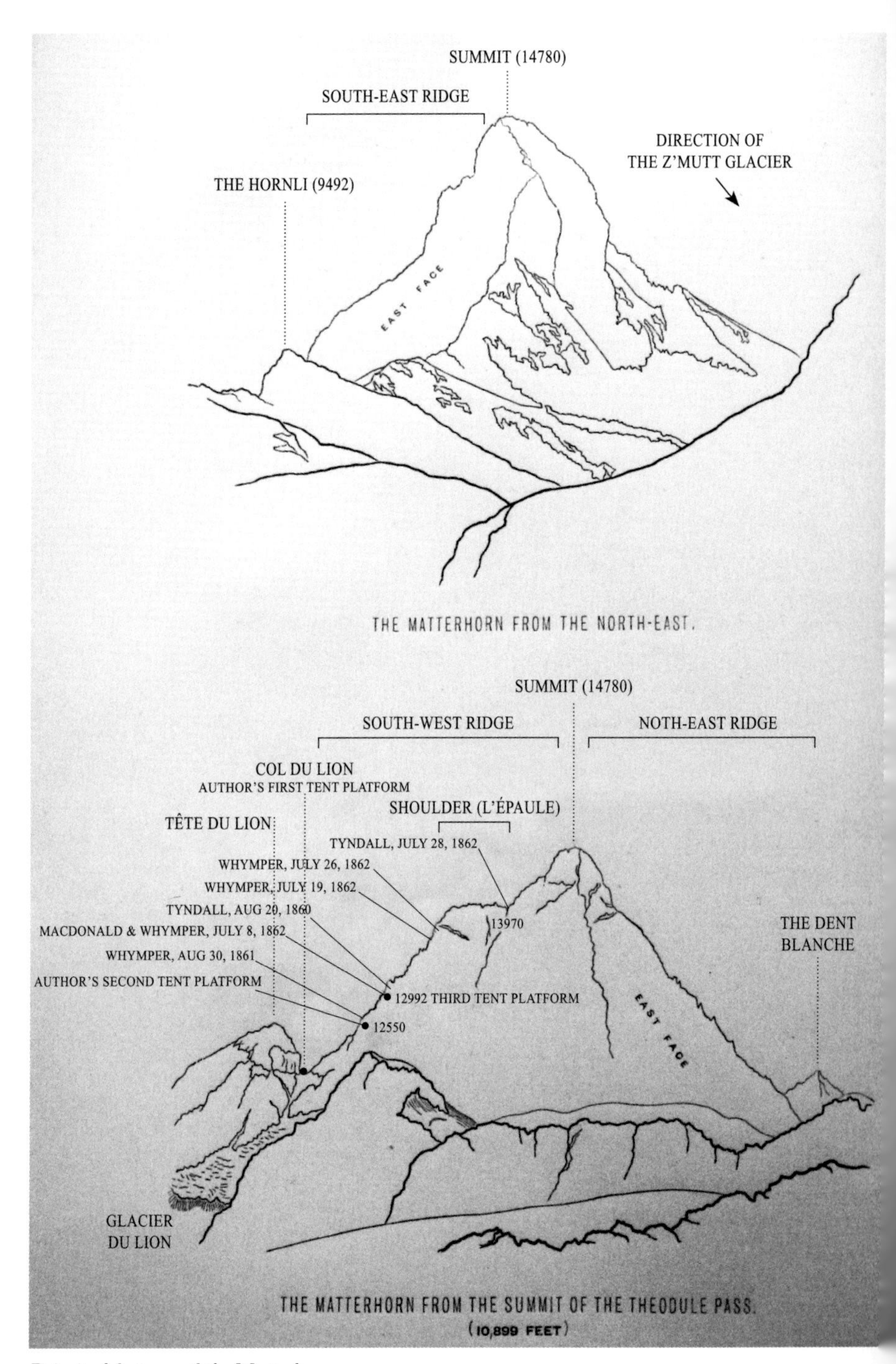
SUMMIT (14780)
SOUTH-EAST RIDGE
DIRECTION OF
THE Z'MUTT GLACIER
THE HORNLI (9492)
EAST FACE
THE MATTERHORN FROM THE NORTH-EAST.
SUMMIT (14780)
SOUTH-WEST RIDGE
NOTH-EAST RIDGE
COL DU LION
AUTHOR'S FIRST TENT PLATFORM
SHOULDER (L'ÉPAULE)
TÊTE DU LION
TYNDALL, JULY 28, 1862
WHYMPER, JULY 26, 1862
WHYMPER, JULY 19, 1862
TYNDALL, AUG 20, 1860
MACDONALD & WHYMPER, JULY 8, 1862
WHYMPER, AUG 30, 1861
AUTHOR'S SECOND TENT PLATFORM
13970
THE DENT
BLANCHE
12992 THIRD TENT PLATFORM
12550
EAST FACE
GLACIER
DU LION
THE MATTERHORN FROM THE SUMMIT OF THE THEODULE PASS.
(10,899 FEET)

Principal features of the Matterhorn

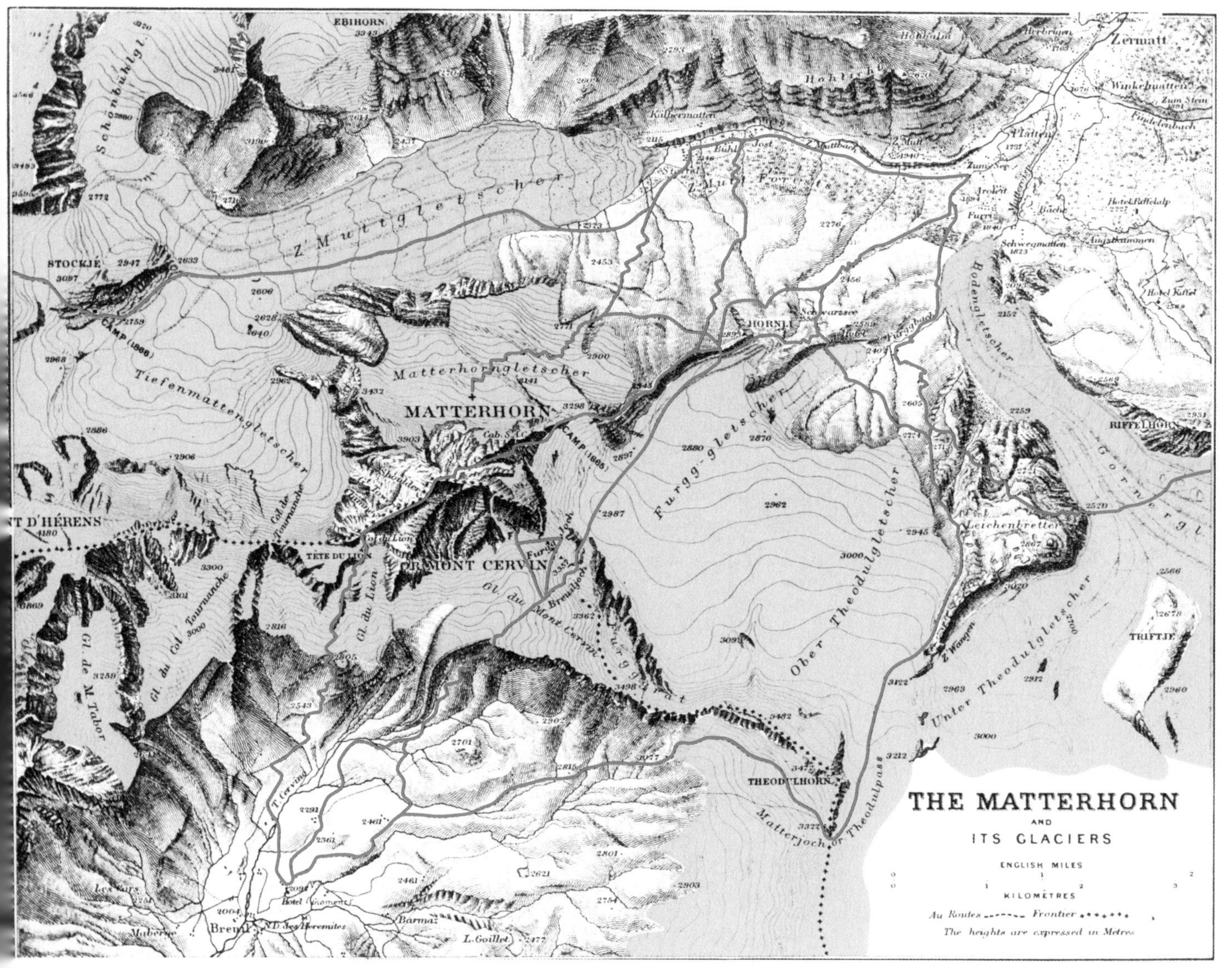

Slide 28: MATTERHORN MAP. This map shows EW's routes 1861 - 65 marked with green lines

With its summit nearly 1800m/6,000ft above, the Matterhorn looks unassailable from the path up from Schwarzsee to the Hörnli Hut. Straight ahead rears the North-East Ridge, the route of EW's first ascent of the mountain. The Hörnli Hut (3260m/10,696ft) originally built in 1899 and from which the ridge is climbed, is obscured by the Hirli crags in the mid-distance. On the left is the East Face and the difficult Furggen (S.E.) Ridge; on the right, the formidable North Face and classic Zmutt (N.W.) Ridge, first climbed in 1879.

The Matterhorn looks equally imposing from whatever side it is seen; it never seems commonplace; and in this respect, and in regard to the impression it makes upon spectators, it stands almost alone amongst mountains. It has no rivals in the Alps, and but few in the world.

Most tourists obtain their first view of the mountain either from the valley of Zermatt, or from that of Tournanche. From the former direction the base of the mountain is seen at its narrowest, and the ridges and faces seem to be of prodigious steepness. The tourist toils up the valley, looking frequently for the great sight which is to reward his pains, without seeing it (for the mountain is first perceived in that direction about a mile to the north of Zermatt), when, all at once, as he turns a rocky corner of the path, it comes into view; not, however, where it is expected; the face has to be raised up to look at it; it seems overhead. Although this is the impression, the fact is that the summit of the Matterhorn from this point makes an angle with the eye of less than 16 degrees, while the Dom, from the same place, makes a larger angle, but is passed by unobserved. So little can dependence be placed on unaided vision.

The view of the mountain from Breil, in the Val Tournanche, is not less striking than that on the other side; but, usually, it makes less impression, because the spectator grows accustomed to the sight while coming up or down the valley. From this direction the mountain is seen to be broken up into a series of pyramidal wedge-shaped masses; on the other side it is remarkable for the large, unbroken extent of cliffs that it presents, and for the simplicity of its outline. It was natural to suppose that a way would more readily be found to the summit on a side thus broken up, than in any other direction. The eastern face, fronting Zermatt, seemed one smooth, impossible cliff, from summit to base; the ghastly precipices which face the Z'mutt glacier forbade any attempt in that direction. There remained only the side of Val Tournanche; and it will be found that nearly all the earliest attempts to ascend the mountain were made on that side.

Slide 29: MATTERHORN AND HORNLI

This is the other side of the Matterhorn – the West Face – a view that greets skiers on the Haute Route as they crest the Col de Valpelline. The Face, notoriously loose and dangerous, was first climbed by William Penhall and his guides via the obvious couloir which bears his name. The Zmutt Ridge forms the left skyline while the right skyline is the South-West or Italian Ridge, attempted so many times by EW and eventually climbed by Carrel and his party three days after EW's success on the opposite side.

This slide gives a good impression of the 'ghastly precipices' facing the Zmutt and Tiefenmatten glaciers which EW found so daunting:

Nothing can seem or be more inaccessible than the Matterhorn upon this side; and even in cold blood one holds the breath when looking at its stupendous cliffs. There are but few equal to them in size in the Alps, and there are none which can more truly be termed *precipices*. Greatest of all of them is the immense north cliff – that which bends over towards the Z'muttgletscher. Stones which drop from the top of that amazing wall fall for about 1500 feet before they touch anything; and those which roll down from above , and bound over it, fall to a much greater depth and leap well nigh 1000 feet beyond its base. This side of the mountain has always seemed sombre – sad – terrible; it is painfully suggestive of decay, ruin and death; and it is now, alas! more than terrible by its associations.

(Here EW must have been referring to the tragic accident that followed his own first ascent in 1865)

Slide 30: THE MATTERHORN FROM THE COL DE VALPELLINE *(from WNW)*

Here the Matterhorn (or Monte Cervino) is seen from the south east on the Swiss/Italian frontier at the Theodul Pass (3290m/10,794ft). On the far side of the craggy South Face is the prominent shoulder or Pic Tyndall. The right skyline, across the snow-covered East Face, is the Hörnli Ridge, its true, relatively benign angle apparent from this direction. The frontier Furggen Ridge separates the two faces.

The Théodule Pass, 10,899 feet, 3322 metres, is the most frequented of the snow passes leading out of the Valley of Zermatt, and perhaps was the first that was discovered. It is easy to traverse, and is useful as a route between the upper Valley of the Rhone and the Valley of Aosta. De Saussure took mules across in 1789, and Ruden said (in 1870) that according to some of the old inhabitants the traffic between Zermatt and Aosta was very considerable. One might see, 'though very seldom, a string of 25 to 30 beasts of burden' crossing it at one time. Cows and mules are still taken over it occasionally. Of late years the glaciers which have to be traversed have shrunk considerably, especially that upon the Italian side. Although crevasses on this route are seldom large, rope should always be employed. I have seen, upon various occasions, Italian peasants crossing alone, provided with no implement except an umbrella. Skeletons of persons unknown are found upon this pass from time to time.

Slide 32: MATTERHORN FROM THE THEODULE

Valtournanche is situated near the head of the valley of the same name which runs northwards from the Aosta valley.

The first efforts to ascend the Matterhorn of which I have heard, were made by the guides, or rather by the chasseurs, of Valtournenche. These attempts were made in the years 1858-9, from the direction of Breil, and the highest point that was attained was about as far as the place which is now called the 'Chimney'.

The Chimney

When EW visited the Italian side of the Matterhorn in the 1890s, he found that rock-falls had completely changed this area, to the extent that the Chimney hardly existed.

Slide 34: VILLAGE OF VALTOURNENCHE

This picture shows the South Face of the Matterhorn with the Col du Lion, the South West Ridge and Pic Tyndall on the left and the Furggen Ridge on the right.

In EW's day, Breuil was a small hamlet located on the Italian side of the Théodule pass above Valtournanche, in a basin leading up to the lower slopes of the Matterhorn. It is now called Cervinia and is a large and flourishing ski resort.

Whymper made six or more attempts on the Matterhorn from the Italian side over the course of five seasons, the first in 1861.

I arrived at Breuil on the 28th of August, with an Oberland guide. On the way up we enquired for another man of all the knowing ones, and they, with one voice, proclaimed that Jean-Antoine Carrel, of the village of Valtournanche, was the cock of the valley. We sought, of course, for Carrel; and found him a well-made, resolute-looking fellow, with a certain defiant air which was rather taking. Yes, he would go. Twenty francs a day, whatever was the result, was his price. I assented. But I must take his comrade. 'Why so?' Oh, it was impossible to get along without another man.' As he said this an evil countenance came forth out of the darkness and proclaimed itself the comrade. I demurred, and the negotiations broke off.

We resolved to go on alone, and anticipating a cold bivouac, begged the loan of a couple of blankets from the innkeeper. He refused them; giving the curious reason, that we had bought a bottle of brandy at Val Tournanche, and had not bought any from him! No brandy, no blankets, appeared to be the rule. We did not require them that night, as it was passed in the highest cow-shed in the valley, which is about an hour nearer to the mountain than the hotel.

When night was coming on, we saw, stealing up the hill-side, the forms of Jean-Antoine Carrel and the comrade. 'Oh ho' I said, 'you have repented?' 'Not at all; you deceive yourself.' 'Why then have you come here?' 'Because we ourselves are going on the mountain tomorrow.' 'Oh, then it is not necessary to have more than three.' 'Not for us.' I admired their pluck, and had a strong inclination to engage the pair; but, finally, decided against it. The comrade turned out to be J.-J. Carrel, nearly related to the other man. Both were bold mountaineers; but Jean-Antoine was incomparably the better man of the two, and was the finest rock-climber I have ever seen.

He was the only man who persistently refused to accept defeat, and who continued to believe, in spite of all discouragements, that the great mountain was not inaccessible, and that it could be ascended from the side of his native valley.

Slide 35: THE MATTERHORN ONE HOUR ABOVE BREIL

This picture illustrates much of the scene of EW's attempts on the Matterhorn South West Ridge 1861-1863. It shows the south west facet of the South Face with the Col du Lion (3580m/11,745ft) just hidden on the far left; the Great Tower is prominent on the South East Ridge – the skyline – which leads up to the Pic Tyndall (4241m/13,914ft). The Matterhorn summit itself, above and beyond, is invisible.

The night wore away without any excitement. The two Carrels crept noiselessly out before daybreak, and went off. We did not leave until nearly seven o'clock, leaving all our properties in the cow-shed; sauntered over the gentian-studded slopes which intervene between the shed and the Glacier du Lion, left cows and their pastures behind, traversed the stony wastes, and arrived at the ice. Old beds of hard snow lay on the right bank (our left hand), and we mounted over them on to the lower portion of the glacier with ease. But, as we ascended, crevasses became numerous, and we were at last brought to a halt by some which were of very large dimensions; and, as our cutting powers were limited, we sought an easier route, and turned, naturally, to the lower rocks of the Tête du Lion, which overlook the glacier on its west. Some good scrambling took us in a short time to the crest of the ridge which descends towards the south; and thence, up to the level of the Col du Lion, there was a long natural staircase, on which it was seldom necessary to use the hands. I dubbed the place 'The Great Staircase'.

Despite this unpromising start to their relationship, EW and Jean-Antoine went on to achieve great things together in later years. Carrel died on the Matterhorn in 1890, at the foot of the Little Staircase, exhausted after an arduous descent in storm conditions.

Such was the end of Jean-Antoine Carrel - a man who was possessed with a pure and genuine love of the mountains; a man of originality and resource, courage and determination, who delighted in exploration. His special qualities marked him out as a fit person to take part in new enterprises, and I preferred him to all others as a companion and assistant upon my journey amongst the Great Andes of the Equator. Going to a new country, on a new continent, he encountered much that was strange and unforeseen; yet when he turned his face homewards he had the satisfaction of knowing that he left no failures behind him.

Jean-Antoine Carrel

Slide 36: MATTERHORN FROM BOTTOM OF LITTLE STAIRCASE

Before the Col du Lion is reached there is an awkward turn to be negotiated. The following year this section proved even more treacherous and EW dubbed it 'Tumble Corner'.

Then the cliffs of the Tête du Lion, which rise above the Couloir, had to be skirted. This part varies considerably in different seasons, and in 1861 we found it difficult; for the fine weather had reduced the snow-beds abutting against it to a lower level than usual, and the rocks which were left exposed at the junction of the snow with the cliffs had few ledges or cracks to which we could hold.

By half-past ten o'clock we stood on the Col, and looked down upon the magnificent basin out of which the Z'Mutt Glacier flows. We decided to pass the night upon the Col, for we were charmed with the capabilities of the place, although it was one where liberties could not be taken. On one side a sheer wall overhung the Tiefenmatten Glacier. On the other, steep, glassy slopes of hard snow descended to the Glacier du Lion, furrowed by water and falling stones. On the north side there was the great peak of the Matterhorn, and on the south the cliffs of the Tête du Lion. Throw a bottle down to the Tiefenmatten - no sound returns for several seconds.

'how fearful
And dizzy 'tis, to cast one's eyes so low!'

But no harm could come from that side. Neither could it from the other. Nor was it likely that it would come from the Tête du Lion, for some jutting ledges overhung our proposed resting-place.

Slide 38: TUMBLE CORNER

Slide 39: COL DU LION

Slide 40: ABOVE THE COL DU LION

This slide shows slabs fallen from the area above the Col du Lion, probably from the feature called the Chimney that EW found in the 1890s so much changed in the thirty years since he first climbed here.

In this picture, looking downwards from a height of about 3880m/12,730ft on the South West Ridge, the Col du Lion below is hidden by the foreground rocks. Beyond the Tête du Lion (3715m/12,188ft) the snowy frontier ridge falls to the Col Tournanche before rising again as the classic, 2 km/1 ¼ mile long East Ridge of the Dent d'Hérens.

In the past winter I had turned my attention to tents, and that which we had brought with us was the result of experiments to devise one which should be sufficiently portable to be taken over the most difficult ground, whilst combining lightness with stability. Its base was just under six feet square, and a cross-section perpendicular to its length was an equilateral triangle, the side of which were six feet long. It was intended to accommodate four persons. It was supported by four ash-poles, six feet and a half long, and one inch and a quarter thick, tapering to the top, which were shod with iron points.

Col du Lion looking towards the Tête du Lion. In the above engraving EW's tent is visible. This was made to his own design.

Whymper's alpine tent

My tent bearer, the hunchback Luc Meynet

EW's tent, restored by the Royal School of Needlework, remains in the care of the Alpine Club.

Slide 42: TETE DU LION

The next section of the ascent presented considerable difficulties demanding unorthodox climbing methods.

"Combined Tactics" were frequently employed by early climbers – obviously steady companions were essential though such methods are not entirely safe. The great pioneering rock climber Owen Glynne Jones was killed while attempting the Ferpècle Arète of the Dent Blanche in 1899 when a 'human pyramid' collapsed.

The ridge above the Great Tower appeared to be the most difficult part of the mountain. One was driven to keep to the edge of the ridge or very near to it; and at the point where we turned back there were smooth walls seven to eight feet high in every direction, which were impassable to a single man, and which could only be surmounted by the assistance of ladders, or by using one's comrades as ladders.

Slide 41: MUTUAL ASSISTANCE

This drawing looking up the South West or Italian Ridge shows the old Refugio Luigi-di-Savoia, built on the site of EW's second tent platform at 3835m/12,580ft. Beyond, fixed ropes lead up to the initial slabs of the Great Tower and the old bivouac hut, the Rifugio Carrel.

This slide appears to have been made from a water-colour sketch, signed 'A.R.Q.' The artist was probably A.R.Quinton (b.1853) who also provided the illustrations for C.L.Freeston's Cycling in the Alps *published in 1900.*

This Great Tower is one of the most striking features of the ridge. It stands out like a turret at the angle of a castle. Behind it a battlemented wall leads upwards to the citadel. Seen from the Théodule Pass it looks only an insignificant pinnacle, but as one approaches it (on the ridge) so it seems to rise, and, when one is at its base, it completely conceals the upper parts of the mountain.

Slide 43: THE GREAT TOWER

This picture is taken from just above the Pic Tyndall and shows the summit block from the Italian side. This point was as far as the photographic expedition in 1893 reached before they had to turn back because of bad weather.

The final 200m/650ft to the summit are seen – rather foreshortened – along the crest of the Shoulder from the Pic Tyndall. The Enjambée gap at the far end of the Shoulder is hidden, but the ledge of the Galerie Carrel is just seen on the left skyline and the position of the Echelle Jordan can be located just below the summit.

The name of this eminence, also referred to as 'The Shoulder' as it hardly justifies being regarded as a separate peak, commemorates the limit of John Tyndall's attempt on the mountain in 1862, the highest point reached up to then. EW was in Breuil at the time.

It was useless to compete with Professor Tyndall and his four men, who were ready to start in a few hours, so I waited to see what would become of their attempt.

Everything seemed to favour it and they set out on a fine morning in high spirits, leaving me tormented with envy and all uncharitableness. If they succeeded, they carried off the prize for which I had so long been struggling; and if they failed, there was no time to make another attempt, for I was due in a few days more in London...

Early next morning some one ran to me saying that a flag was seen on the summit of the Matterhorn. It was not so, however, although I saw that they had passed where we had turned back [some days earlier]. I had now no doubt of their final success, for they had got beyond the point which Carrel, not less than myself, had always considered to be the most questionable place on the whole mountain.

But success had also eluded Tyndall:

The sun had set before the men were descried coming over the pastures. There was no spring in their steps – they, too, were defeated. The Carrels hid their heads, and the others said, as men will do when they have been beaten, that the mountain was horrible, impossible, and so forth. Professor Tyndall told me that they had arrived within a stone's throw of the summit, and admonished me to have nothing more to do with the mountain.

The problem turned out to have been a notch on the ridge which was impossible to pass using the approach the party had chosen.

Slide 44: MATTERHORN FROM THE SHOULDER

Whymper made his third attempt to reach the summit on his own on 3rd July 1862. It nearly ended in disaster on the way down.

The Col du Lion was passed, and fifty yards more would have placed me on the 'Great Staircase,' down which one can run. But on arriving at an angle of the cliffs of the Tête du Lion, while skirting the upper edge of the snow which abuts against them, I found that the heat of the two past days had nearly obliterated the steps which had been cut while coming up. The rocks happened to be impracticable just at this corner, and it was necessary to make the steps afresh. The snow was too hard to beat or tread down, and at the angle it was all but ice; half-a-dozen steps only were required, and then the ledges could be followed again. So I held to the rock with my right hand, and prodded at the snow with the point of my stick until a good step was made, and then, leaning round the angle, did the same for the other side. So far well, but in attempting to pass the corner I slipped and fell.

In attempting the corner I slipped

The slope was steep on which this took place, and was at the top of a gully that led down through two subordinate buttresses towards the Glacier du Lion - which was just seen, a thousand feet below. The gully narrowed and narrowed, until there was a mere thread of snow lying between two walls of rock, which came to an abrupt termination at the top of a precipice that intervened between it and the glacier. Imagine a funnel cut in half through its length, placed at an angle of 45 degrees, with its point below and its concave side uppermost, and you will have a fair idea of the place.

Slide 46: TUMBLE CORNER AGAIN

The knapsack brought my head down first, and I pitched into some rocks about a dozen feet below; they caught something and tumbled me off the edge, head over heels, into the gully; the bâton was dashed from my hands, and I whirled downwards in a series of bounds, each longer than the last; now over ice, now into rocks; striking my head four or five times, each time with increased force. The last bound sent me spinning through the air, in a leap of fifty or sixty feet, from one side of the gully to the other, and I struck the rocks, luckily, with the whole of my left side. They caught my clothes for a moment, and I fell back on to the snow with motion arrested. My head fortunately came the right side up, and a few frantic catches brought me to a halt, in the neck of the gully, and on the verge of the precipice. Bâton, hat and veil skimmed by and disappeared, and the crash of the rocks - which I had started - as they fell on to the glacier, told how narrow had been the escape from utter destruction. As it was, I fell nearly 200 feet in seven or eight bounds. Ten feet more would have taken me in one gigantic leap of 800 feet on to the glacier below.

The Great Gulley on the south-east of the Italian side of the Matterhorn was considered as a possible route until exploration in June 1865 revealed that it is continually subject to stone-fall, as can be seen from the tracks in the snow in Slide 47.

The Matterhorn South Face takes the sun and the rock is notoriously unstable, rendering such places as the Great Gulley death traps except in rarely perfect winter conditions.

While the men were unpacking the food I went to a little promontory to examine our proposed route more narrowly, and to admire our noble couloir, which led straight up into the heart of the mountain for fully one thousand feet. It then bent towards the north, and ran up to the crest of the south eastern ridge. My curiosity was piqued to know what was round this corner, and whilst I was gazing up at it, and following with the eye the exquisitely drawn curves which wandered down the snow in the gulley, all converging to a large rut in its centre, I saw a few little stones skidding down. I consoled myself with thinking that they would not interfere with us if we adhered to the side. But then a larger one came down, a solitary fellow, rushing at the rate of sixty miles an hour – and another – and another. I was unwilling to raise the fears of the men unnecessarily, and said nothing to them.

A cannonade on the Matterhorn

Arnold Lunn described this as 'the silliest of all conceivable routes…one of the strangest aberrations in Alpine history. This joint attempt by Whymper, Croz and Almer is a classic example of the fallibility of experts, for the most inexperienced of novices could hardly have picked a worse route.'

They did not hear the stones. Almer was seated on a rock, carving large slices from the leg of mutton, the others were chatting, and the first intimation they had of danger was from a crash - a sudden roar - which reverberated awfully amongst the cliffs, and, looking up, they saw masses of rocks, boulders and stones, big and little, dart around the corner 800 feet or so above us, fly with fearful fury against the opposite cliffs, rebound from them against the walls on our side, and descend; some ricocheting

Slide 47: THE GREAT GULLEY

from side to side in a frantic manner; some bounding down in leaps of 100 feet or more over the snow; and more trailing down in a jumbled, confused mass, mixed with snow and ice, deepening the grooves which, a moment before, had excited my admiration.

The men looked wildly around for protection, and, dropping the food, dashed under cover in all directions. The precious mutton was pitched on one side, the wine bag was let fall, and its contents gushed out from the unclosed neck, while all four cowered under defending rocks, endeavouring to make themselves as small as possible.

Reflected in the Riffelsee, the little tarn on the Riffelberg, this is a favourite view of the Matterhorn. The East Face, appearing much steeper than it is, is bounded on the left by the frontier Furggen Ridge and on the right by the Hörnli Ridge, its lower crest confused here by the Zmutt Ridge beyond.

By 1865 Whymper had become convinced that the south-west ridge, on the Italian side of the mountain, did not offer the greatest chance of success, not least because he observed that the East Face was nothing like as steep as most people thought.

When one looks at the Matterhorn from Zermatt, the mountain is regarded (nearly) from the north-east. The face that fronts the east is consequently neither seen in profile nor in full front, but almost half-way between the two; it looks, therefore, more steep than it really is. The majority of those who visit Zermatt go up to the Riffelberg, or to the Gornergrat, and from these places the mountain naturally looks still more precipitous, because its eastern face (which is almost all that is seen of it) is viewed more directly in front. From the Riffel hotel the slope seems to be set at an angle of 70 degrees.

Several years passed away before I shook myself clear of my early and false impressions regarding the steepness of this side of the Matterhorn. First of all, I noticed that there were places on this eastern face where the snow remained permanently all the year round. I do not speak of snow in gullies, but of considerable slopes which are about half-way up the face. Such beds as these could not continue to remain throughout the summer, unless the snow had been able to accumulate during the winter in large masses, in a situation such as this, at angles much exceeding 45 degrees. Hence I was bound to conclude that the eastern face was many degrees removed from perpendicularity; and, to be sure on this point, I went to the slopes between the Z'Muttgletscher and the Matterhorngletscher, above the chalets of Staffel, whence the face could be seen in profile.

Matterhorn from beyond Staffel, Hörnli ridge to the left

Its appearance from this direction is amazing to those who have only seen it from the east. It looks so totally different from the apparently sheer and perfectly unclimbable cliff one sees from the Riffelberg, that it is hard

Slide 49: THE MATTERHORN AND THE RIFFEL LAKE

to believe the two slopes are one and the same thing. Its angle scarcely exceeds 40 degrees.

EW also discovered another reason for abandoning the south-west ridge:

A more serious hindrance to mounting the south-west ridge is found in the dip of its rocks to the west-south-west. The great mass of the Matterhorn is composed of regularly stratified rocks which rise towards the east, so that the rocks on some portions of the ridge leading from the Col du Lion towards the summit dip outwards, and fractured edges overhang. This is shown in the annexed diagram, Fig.A. It will be readily understood that such an arrangement is not favourable for climbers. Once persuaded that structure and not texture was the real impediment, it was reasonable to infer that the opposite side, that is to say the eastern face, might be comparatively easy. In brief, that an arrangement should be found like Fig.B, instead of like Fig.A. This trivial deduction was the key to the ascent of the Matterhorn.

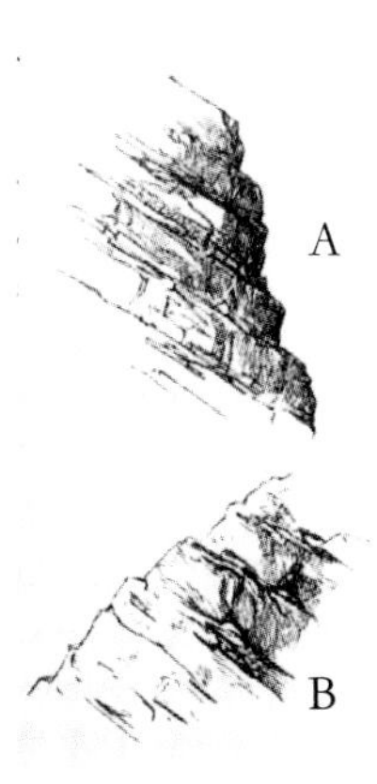

In July 1865 EW decided to make an attempt on the Matterhorn from the Zermatt side. A most important member of the party was his old guide Michel Croz from le Tour in the Chamonix valley, with whom he had made many first ascents.

Croz was happiest when he was employing his powers to the utmost. Places where you and I would 'toil and sweat, and yet be freezing cold,' were bagatelles to him, and it was only when he got above the range of ordinary mortals, and was required to employ his magnificent strength, and to draw upon his unsurpassed knowledge of ice and snow, that he could be said to be really and truly happy.

Of all the guides with whom I travelled, Michel Croz was the man who was most after my own heart. He did not work like a blunt razor, and take to his toil unkindly. He did not need urging, or to be told a second time to do anything. You had but to say *what* was to be done, and *how* it was to be done, and the work *was* done, if it was possible. Such men are not common, and when they are known they are valued. Michel was not widely known, but those who knew him came again and again. The inscription that is placed upon his tomb truthfully records the he was 'beloved by his comrades and esteemed by travellers.'

Slide 48: MICHEL CROZ

EW takes up the story:

We started from Zermatt on the 13th of July 1865, at half-past 5, on a brilliant and perfectly cloudless morning. We were eight in number – Croz, old Peter Taugwalder and his two sons [Zermatt guide and porters], Lord Francis Douglas, Douglas Hadow [young and inexperienced], the Rev. Charles Hudson [considered by the mountaineering fraternity to be the best amateur of his time] and I.

Lord Francis Douglas

Revd. Charles Hudson

To ensure steady motion, one tourist and one native walked together. The youngest Taugwalder fell to my share, and the lad marched well, proud to be on the expedition, and happy to shew his powers. The wine-bags also fell to my lot to carry, and throughout the day, after each drink, I replenished them secretly with water, so that at the next halt they were found fuller than before! This was considered a good omen, and little short of miraculous.

EW's party bivouacked at mid-day on a good ledge at about 3818m/12,526ft, whence the route led them off the Ridge onto the East Face. The line rejoins the Ridge at the Solvay Hut at 4003m/13,133ft via the steep slabs known as the Moseleyplatte where a Mr. Moseley, an American climber, was killed in 1879. Slide 62 shows the view of the steep summit pyramid from the easy but treacherous terrain shortly below the Moseley slabs.

Whilst the party made camp, Croz and young Peter went on to see what was above, bringing back good news:
'Not a single difficulty! We could have gone to the summit and returned today easily!'

Next morning, success seemed within their grasp:
We assembled together outside the tent before dawn on the morning of the 14th and started directly it was light enough to move. Young Peter came on with us as a guide, and his brother returned to Zermatt. We followed the route which had been taken on the previous day, and in a few minutes turned the rib which had intercepted the view of the eastern face from our tent platform. The whole of the great slope was now revealed, rising for 3000 feet like a huge natural staircase. Some parts of it were more, some less, easy; but we were not once brought to a halt by any serious impediment, for when an obstruction was met in front it could always be turned to the right or to the left. For the greater part of the way, there was, indeed, no occasion for the rope, and sometimes Hudson led, sometimes myself. At 6.20 we had attained a height of 12,800 feet, and halted for half-an-hour; we then continued the ascent without a break until 9.55, when we stopped for fifty minutes at a height of 14,000 feet.

We had now arrived at the foot of that part which, from Zermatt, seems perpendicular or overhanging, and could no longer continue on the eastern side.For a little distance we ascended by snow upon the arête – that is, the crest of the ridge – descending towards Zermatt, and then, by common consent, turned over to the right, or to the northern side. Before doing so we made a change in the order of ascent. Croz went first, I followed, Hudson came third; Hadow and old Peter were last. 'Now,' said Croz, as he led off, 'now for something altogether different.' The work became difficult and required caution. In some places there was little to hold, and it was desirable that those should be in front who were least likely to slip. The general slope of the mountain at this part was less than 40 degrees, and snow had accumulated in, and had filled up, the interstices of the rock face, leaving only occasional fragments projecting here and there. These were at times covered with a thin film of ice, produced from the melting and refreezing of the snow. It was a place over which any fair mountaineer might pass in safety, and Mr Hudson ascended this part, and so far as I know, the entire mountain, without having the slightest assistance rendered to him on any occasion.

Slide 62: THE MATTERHORN-SUMMIT SEEN FROM HALF-WAY UP THE FACE

The summit

Sometimes, after I had taken a hand from Croz, or received a pull, I turned to offer the same to Hudson; but he invariably declined, saying it was not necessary. Mr Hadow, however, was not accustomed to this kind of work, and required continual assistance. It is only fair to say that the difficulty which he found at this part arose simply and entirely from want of experience.

This solitary difficult part was of no great extent. We bore away over it at first, nearly horizontally, for a distance of about 400 feet; then ascended directly towards the summit for about 60 feet; and then doubled back to the ridge which descends towards Zermatt. A long stride round a rather awkward corner brought us to snow once more. The last doubt vanished! The Matterhorn was ours! Nothing but 200 feet of easy snow remained to be surmounted!

On the way down, however, a slip had tragic consequences. Not long after the party had started their descent:

...a sharp-eyed lad ran into the Monte Rosa hotel, to Seiler, saying that he had seen an avalanche fall from the summit of the Matterhorn on to the Matterhorngletscher. The boy was reproved for telling idle stories; he was right, nevertheless, and this was what he saw:

Michel Croz had laid down his axe, and in order to give Hadow greater security, was absolutely taking hold of his legs, and putting his feet, one by one, into their proper positions. So far as I know, no-one was actually descending. I cannot speak with certainty, because the two leading men were partially hidden from my sight by an intervening mass of rock, but it is my belief, from the movements of their shoulders, that Croz, having done as I have said, was in the act of turning round, to go down a step or two himself; at this moment Mr. Hadow slipped, fell against him, and knocked him over. I heard one startled exclamation from Croz, then saw him and Mr. Hadow flying downwards; in another moment Hudson was dragged from his steps, and Lord F. Douglas immediately after him.

Gustave Doré *The Fall*

All this was the work of a moment. Immediately we heard Croz's exclamation, old Peter and I planted ourselves as firmly as the rocks would permit; the rope was taut between us, and the jerk came on us both as one man. We held; but the rope broke midway between Taugwalder and Lord Francis Douglas.

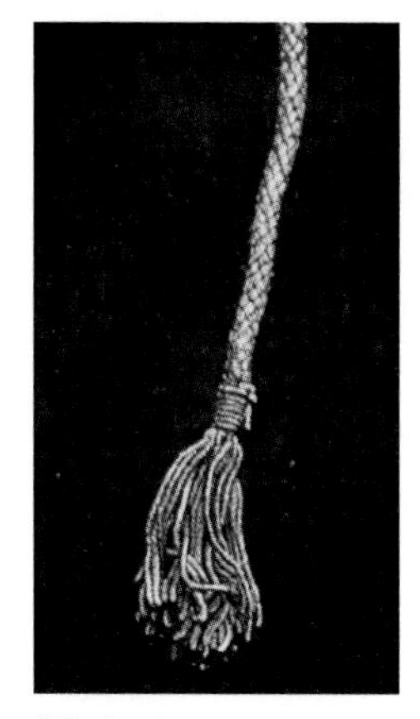

The broken rope

For a few seconds we saw our unfortunate companions sliding downwards on their backs, and spreading out their hands, endeavouring to save themselves. They passed from our sight uninjured, disappeared one by one, and then fell from precipice to precipice on to the Matterhorngletscher below, a distance of nearly 4000 feet in height. From the moment the rope broke it was impossible to help them.

So perished our comrades!

So the traditional inaccessibility of the Matterhorn was vanquished, and was replaced by legends of a more real character. Others will essay to scale its proud cliffs, but to none will it be the mountain it was to its early explorers. Others may tread its summit-snows, but none will ever know the feelings of those who first gazed upon its marvellous panorama: and none, I trust, will ever be compelled to tell of joy turned into grief, and of laughter into mourning. It proved to be a stubborn foe; it resisted long, and gave many a hard blow; it was defeated at last with an ease that none could have anticipated, but, like a relentless enemy - conquered but not crushed - it took terrible vengeance.

EW devotes the second half of his lecture to the area around Mont Blanc.

One of the earliest accounts of the Mont Blanc region dates from 1741-2, resulting from an exchange of letters between an Englishman, William Windham, and a Swiss, Pierre Martel. This is the first time we meet the current name for the mountain.

I have been unable to learn that the name Mont Blanc has been printed at an earlier date. It would seem, therefore, under any circumstances, that it came into use somewhere about the time of Martel's visit. Possibly, it was invented to satisfy inquisitive visitore demanding 'what do you call this?' and 'what do you call that?' Some of the Aiguilles had been christened already. The Dru, the Charmoz, the Blaitière and Mont Mally were established names in 1742; and I imagine that, perhaps, when Martel pursued his inquiries, and pointing to the great snowy dome demanded 'and what do you call that?' the Chamoniards replied simply, 'Oh! We call that the white mountain,' without intending him to suppose that this was an established appellation. Down went Mont Blanc in his notes, and the name has stuck to the mountain ever since.

Slide 50: MAP OF MONT BLANC
Outlined in green are some of the routes EW describes, including the usual route to the summit in his day, from Chamonix via the Grands Mulets as well as the path to Montenvers and the Mer de Glace.

De Saussure reached the summit of Mont Blanc in 1787.

Chamonix speedily benefited from the publicity which was given to it by the circulation of Windham and Martel's letters. It soon became the fashion to visit the Glacières.

Amongst those who went there was a young man named Horace Benedict de Saussure. He belonged to an old Swiss family, settled a few miles from Geneva. Whenever he walked abroad, the Great White Mountain must have caught his eye, on the other side of the lake. De Saussure was a man of studious habits, and at the early age of twenty-two became a Professor of Philosophy at the Academy of Geneva. 'As for me,' he says in his Travels, 'I had from my infancy a most decided passion for mountains. In 1760,
I went alone and on foot to visit the Glaciers of Chamonix. I returned again the next season, and since then I have not allowed a year to pass without making journeys to the mountains for the sake of study.'

He said that so early as 1760 and 1761 he had it proclaimed in the three parishes of the valley of Chamonix that he would give a considerable reward to anyone who should discover a practicable way to the top of the Great White Mountain, and that he would even pay for their time if their attempts were unsuccessful. It does not appear, from aught we know, that anyone even contemplated the ascent of Mont Blanc before this reward was offered; or that any of the peaks of Mont Blanc had been ascended at that time, or that the Chamoniards in general were entitled to be considered mountaineers.

Slide 51: PORTRAIT OF DE SAUSSURE

The asterisks mark sites of overnight bivouacs

This is the northern, French, flank of Mont Blanc (4808m/15,774ft) taken with a long-focus lens from the Brévent on the opposite side of the Arve valley. The sharp peaklet at the bottom left, above the Grands Mulets rocks, is the Pic Wilson, the altitude of which, 3266m/10,715ft, gives some idea of the scale.

The ice-filled cwm is the Grand Plateau with the crags of the Rochers Rouges, Inférieurs and Supérieurs, above. The Ancien Passage, line of the 1786 first ascent, is the ice ramp trending leftwards between these rocks.

The Vallot refuge/observatory, constructed in 1890, is just visible below rocks on the skyline, top right.

The view of Mont Blanc from the Brévent is the finest near one that can be had on this side. The best point for seeing the routes which are ordinarily taken is about half-way up, between Bel-Achat and the top. Mont Blanc looks at its best under afternoon light (after 3.30 p.m.)

Mont Blanc from the Brévent

Slide 52: MONT BLANC FROM THE BREVENT

Always jealous of their calling, the Chamonix Guides operated a closed shop with a fixed tariff, working out of this same office until the 1960s.

In a diary entry in July 1893 EW wrote:

Visited Guide Chief to ask his permission to allow me a guide and five porters for Mont Blanc. He graciously allowed me.

His treatment was rather worse after the first ascent of the Aiguille Verte, in 1865

We halted at the inn to get a little food, and at a quarter past eight re-entered Chamonix, amidst firing of cannon and other demonstrations of satisfaction on the part of the hotel-keepers.

One would have thought the ascent of this mountain, which had been frequently assailed before without success, would have afforded some gratification to a population whose chief support is derived from tourists, and that the prospect of the perennial flow of francs which might be expected to result from it would have stifled the jealousy consequent on the success of foreigners.

It was not so. Chamounix stood on its rights. A stranger had ignored their regulations, had imported two foreign guides, and, furthermore, he had added injury to that insult - he had not taken a single Chamounix guide. Chamounix would be revenged! It would bully the foreign guides; it would tell them they had lied, - they had not made the ascent! Where were their proofs? Where was the flag upon the summit?

There were the materials for a very pretty riot; but they manage these things better in France than we do, and the gendarmes - three strong - came down and dispersed the crowd. The guides quailed before the cocked hats. And retired to cabarets to take little glasses of absinthe and other liquors more or less injurious to human health.

Slide 53: BUREAU DES GUIDES

This picture, shot due southwards from the vicinity of La Flégère, shows Chamonix as a small village standing at some 1030m/3380ft beside the Arve river. The summit of Mont Blanc is to the left of centre at the top and the pointed peak with dark ridges to the right of centre is the Aiguille de Gôuter (3845m/12,615ft). Below this, to the left, between the Bossons and the Taconnaz Glaciers, is the ridge known as the Montagne de la Côte. In EW's day the Bossons Glacier reached almost down to the road and has retreated some 300m/1,000ft since.

Most of the normal route taken by the guides to the summit in those days is visible in the picture: up the Montagne de la Côte, across the confused area of ice known as La Jonction to the Grands Mulets rocks and hut, continuing across the Grand Plateau, to the Corridor below the Rochers Rouges. EW clearly took the view that the Guides' charges were exorbitant.

The Chamonix Tarif for Mont Blanc is 100 francs per Guide. If two are taken by a single individual, and a night is passed at the Grands Mulets, the total cost will be little if at all under £12.

It is to be noted that the Chamonix Tarif takes various contingencies into consideration. If the tourist starts for Mont Blanc and gets no higher than the Grands Mulets, he will be charged 20 francs only, if he returns within one day. If he gets to the Grand Plateau, the charge will be 50 francs; to the top of the Corridor, or to the top of the Bosses, 70 francs. If he goes higher than these points the full 100 francs may be exacted. If the ascent occupies more than three days, each guide must be paid 10 francs extra per day.

The prices at the Grands Mulets are high, and the food indifferent. Economy can be effected by taking provisions from Chamonix instead of buying them at the Grands Mulets; but this course is not looked upon favourably by Chamonix Guides, or at the Grands Mulets.

Slide 54: MONT BLANC FROM CHAMONIX

The ridge called the Montagne de la Côte lies between the Glacier de Taconnaz (to the west or right) and the Glacier des Bossons (to the east).

Slide 55: MONT BLANC SHOWING MONTAGNE DE LA COTE

The usual route to the summit of Mont Blanc in EW's time was via the Pierre Pointue.

The mule-path comes to an end there, but thence to what is called the Pierre à l'Echelle there is a path over which any English boy ought to be able to go alone. After that he had better have someone with him. The way from the Pierre Pointue to Pierre à l'Echelle gradually approaches the right bank of the Glacier des Bossons, and at the latter place arrives at the edge of the ice. There are not many ladders usually seen there now. It takes its name from the habit which was formerly indulged in, in imitation of De Saussure, of carrying a ladder about to use for crossing crevasses. The ladder, or ladders, were usually left here. From this place the rocks called the Grands Mulets can be seen, and in clear weather anyone who is accustomed to traverse glaciers will find a route to them; but in bad weather this passage, though scarcely a mile and a half long, is trying even to experts. There have been occasions when it has been impossible to the élite of the guides of Chamonix. For one-half of the distance there are no greater difficulties than such as arise from walking over ice which is fissured; but upon arrival at 'the junction' - the point of union of the eastern Glacier de Taconnaz and the Glacier des Bossons - the ice is a good deal dislocated, under any circumstances will require the use of the axe, and at times requires something more. The excursion from Chamonix to the Grands Mulets ought not to be undertaken without guides except by persons who are accustomed to traverse glaciers under all conditions of weather.

Slide 56: THE JUNCTION
La Jonction, where several glacier streams flatten out and collide at around 3000m/9,800ft is an area of tortured ice and séracs that is awkward to cross.

Matthias Zurbriggen (1855-1917), who came from Macugnaga on the Italian side of Monte Rosa, was one of the most-travelled of the guides of this period, having visited the Andes and the Himalayas. Earlier in 1894 he had joined Sir Martin, later Lord, Conway in part of the journey that was to result in the book, 'The Alps from End to End'.
In an obituary, Conway wrote:

'He was by nature ambitious of attainment. He desired to acquire every sort of kind of knowledge and every sort of skill he could come by. Ultimately, he could speak English, French, German, Italian, a little Spanish and (when in India) a smattering of Hindustani. He was also a competent blacksmith, a good carpenter, a useful all round man with his hands, and a most accomplished craftsman with axe and rope on the mountainside. He was passionate, extravagant, lusty and overflowing. He was a very hard worker and unrestrained in his relaxations. He was easy to get on with if taken the right way, and just as easy to quarrel with.'

In 1894, when making an ascent of Mont Blanc by this route, I occupied the same length of time as De Saussure - three hours - over this section, though led by such good icemen as Daniel Maquignaz and Matthias Zurbriggen.

Slide 57: PORTRAIT OF ZURBRIGGEN

The 1894 party is seen here taking a break in the shelter of the boulders, including Paul Breton, Daniel Maquignaz, Matthias Zurbriggen and Aloys Pollinger. Zurbriggen seems to be living up to his reputation as a man of strong views.

These boulders, at 2530m/8,300ft, close to the ice below La Jonction, provided shelter for the night for the local chamois hunter, Jacques Balmat, and Paccard, the village doctor, in the course of the first ascent of Mont Blanc. The place has since become known as Le Gîte à Balmat.

About 200 feet below [the top of the Montagne de la Côte] there are some very large boulders, which appear to have come from the Rochers Rouges. One of them measures 10 metres high, by 9 by 14 metres. From the summit one sees the Grands Mulets, and the way up Mont Blanc as far as the edge of the Grand Plateau. The Aig. du Midi and the Dome du Gouter both look very fine from this position, and the view over the valley of Chamonix is as good as, or better than that from the Grands Mulets.

Slide 58: BOULDERS ON THE MONTAGNE DE LA COTE

Seen from the right bank of the Bossons Glacier near the Pierre à l'Échelle rock, at about 2550m/8,350ft, on the usual route to the Grands Mulets Hut, this picture looks south west across the broken ice of La Jonction, towards the rock peaklets of the Grands Mulets and Pic Wilson with the Dôme du Goûter (4304m/14,121ft) rising beyond.

After passing 'the junction,' the way becomes easier; but it is seldom possible to steer a *direct* course to the Grands Mulets. One is driven to the right (north-west), and then has to double back.

The Grands Mulets, 10,113 feet, as a resting place on the ascent of Mont Blanc, was discovered by the earliest explorers of the mountain. This island of rock is, doubtless, an Aiguille of the ridge which lower down is called the Montagne de la Côte. It occupies a very commanding position, and the views from it looking across the Valley of Chamonix, towards the Aiguille du Midi, and, in the contrary direction, over the Glacier de Taconnaz to the Aiguille du Goûter are all striking. A sunset from the Grands Mulets will be remembered.

Slide 60: THE WAY TO THE GRAND MULETS

Albert Smith described the sunset, seen from the Grands Mulets, on his 1851 ascent:

The sun at length went down behind the Aiguille du Gouté, and then, for two hours, a scene of such wild and wondrous beauty – of such inconceivable and unearthly splendour – burst upon me, that, spell-bound, and almost trembling with the emotion its magnificence called forth – with every sense, and feeling, and thought absorbed by its brilliancy, I saw far more than the realization of the most gorgeous visions that opium or hasheesh could evoke, accomplished. At first, everything about us, above, around, below – the sky, the mountain, and the lower peaks – appeared one uniform creation of burnished gold, so brightly dazzling, that, now our veils were removed, the eye could scarcely bear the splendour. As the twilight gradually crept over the lower world, the glow became still more vivid; and presently, as the blue mists rose in the valleys, the tops of the higher mountains looked like islands rising from a filmy ocean – an archipelago of gold. By degrees this metallic lustre was softened into tints, first orange, then bright, transparent crimson, along the horizon, rising through the different hues with prismatic regularity, until immediately above us, the sky was a deep, pure blue, merging towards the east into glowing violet.

Albert Smith (1816 - 1860)

Slide 59: SUNSET FROM THE MONTAGNE DE LA COTE

The building there - termed the Pavilion - is, like the other one at the Pierre Pointue, the property of the Commune of Chamonix, and the two places are generally let together for a term of years. There are beds at the Grands Mulets, and food can be had. 'The Commune reserves to itself the right to fix the price of lodging, etc.,' - the tenant has no option in this matter.

This highly dramatic view of the Grands Mulets Hut (3051m/10,010ft) and its surroundings appears in Albert Smith's account of his 1851 ascent of the mountain.

Slide 61: THE GRANDS MULETS

Slide 62: VIEW FROM THE GRANDS MULETS
The view from the hut looking over the upper Taconnaz glacier towards the Aiguille du Goûter

When this picture was taken, in 1894, the Aiguille du Midi (3842m/12,605ft) had not yet been disfigured by the cable-car station that opened in 1955. The modern tourist télèphérique station is tunnelled into the lower, left hand summit and a bridge leads to galleries in the main peak. This shot was taken with a telephoto lens from somewhere in the vicinity of the Gîte à Balmat and shows the upper part of the West Face.

The Aiguille du Midi was first ascended in August, 1856, by Alexandre Devouassoux and Ambroise Simond (guides) and by Jean Simond, a boy of seventeen (porter), who were employed by the Count Fernand de Bouillé. Twenty-four metres below the summit, the Count and the rest of his party were left behind, while the three went up. They were away for an hour, and upon returning flatly refused to conduct their employer to the summit. Said Devouassoux, amongst other things, 'Monsieur le comte, your flag floats above, the ascent is made; but for all the riches of the world I won't be going up again .' Said Simond, 'There's not one of you capable of going there without losing his life. My spirit may go there perhaps after my death, but may body never. The business is over - no one shall compel me to go there again.' It was rather hard on the Count, who had taken eight guides and porters, and a miner, on the occasion, and had made several other attempts to ascend the Aiguille.

Slide 64: THE AIGUILLE DU MIDI

This is actually the little Aiguille du Roc (3409m/12,605ft), an eastern subsidiary feature of the Grépon, first climbed, with difficulty, long after EW's day. The picture was taken from the vicinity of the Col des Nantillons, with the Aiguille Verte rising in the distance.

EW has little to say about the Grépon itself.

First climbed in the 1880's - height uncertain, about 3482 metres.

The first ascent of the Grépon was by A.F.Mummery with the Swiss guides Burgener and Venetz in 1881. EW and Mummery never saw eye to eye, and this may be the reason why EW gave such short shrift in his Chamonix guidebook to a remarkable achievement. The crux of the route is what is known to this day as the Mummery Crack.

Writing in 1895, Mummery said: 'It has frequently been noticed that all mountains appear doomed to pass through the three stages: An inaccessible peak – The most difficult ascent in the Alps – An easy day for a lady. I must confess that the Grépon has not yet reached this final stage.' *His reference to the final stage is not quite as politically incorrect as it might seem: the lady in question was Lily Bristow who accompanied Mummery and Slingsby on the second traverse of the Grépon, in 1893, and* 'showed the representatives of the Alpine Club the way in which steep rocks should be climbed.'

Slide 65: THE AIGUILLE DU GREPON (incorrectly titled by EW)

Slide 66: THE AIGUILLE DU GEANT

One of the most spectacular peaks in the massif, the Aiguille (or Dent) du Géant (4013m/13,166ft), is a frontier peak, seen here from the snowfields just below the Col de Rochefort. A one-time 'last great problem', it repulsed several powerful attempts – even one with a rocket and rope. Eventually the slightly lower of the two summits was reached in 1882 by the Italian party, as described, and a month later W.W.Graham and his guides reached the higher top.

The Aiguille du Géant is perhaps one of the few pinnacles which it is impossible to ascend by fair climbing. In 1871, when regarding it from the summit of Mont Mallet, Mr Leslie Stephen thought, 'Nobody will ever get up that peak by fair means. Of course, it is impossible to say what may not be within the resources of the engineer's art; but without stooping to some of those artifices which the mountaineer regards with the horror aroused in regard to other pursuits by the epithet 'unsportsmanlike,' no one, I venture to say with unusual confidence, will ever climb the Dent du Géant.'

It was first ascended by MM. Alessandro, Corradino, Alfonso (17 years old) and Gaudenzio Sella, with the guides J-J. Maquignaz, B. Maquignaz and Daniel Maquignaz of Val Tournanche, on July 29, 1882. Before the ascent was made, the guides worked four days in mining the rock, and driving in iron stanchions to which ropes were attached.

It was Jaques Balmat who, in 1786, first discovered this section of the route to the summit of Mont Blanc known as the Ancien Passage, which he followed with Dr Paccard in the successful ascent of Mont Blanc later the same year. Balmat describes his experience on the mountain after he had been left on his own by others of his party.

The line of the third ascent, the ice ramp of the Ancien Passage Supérieur, is clearly seen in this picture taken across the Grand Plateau (from about 3970m/13,000ft). Known as the Voie Saussure, it was pioneered by de Saussure, Balmat and eighteen guides to become the 'voie normale' of the early years. The two previous ascents had taken the Ancien Passage Inférieur, a similar ice ramp on the far side of the rock band, the Rochers Rouges Supérieurs, on the left.

'I found myself alone,' said he, 'and was divided between a wish to rejoin the others, and an ambition to attempt the ascent alone. I was piqued at being left behind, and something told me that, this time, I should succeed.' He decided on the latter course; descended on to a great snowy plain that is about 2600 feet below the summit (the Grand Plateau), and remounted by the exceedingly steep snow which is on the right, digging out footsteps with the point of his baton, until high enough to see all the rest of the way clear to the top. 'It wasn't either easy or amusing, I can tell you, to be hung up, so to speak, on one leg, with an abyss underneath, and obliged to fashion this sort of staircase. But at last I got to the Rocher Rouge. Oh! I am there, I said. There was nothing more to hinder one - no more steps to make.' Night was approaching, there were clouds about, and he did not try to go to the top - less from fear of losing himself than from conviction that he would not be seen, and that no one would believe he had been there.

The above account, received wisdom in EW's day, is now widely thought to have been a boast by Balmat to make him more likely to win de Saussure's prize.

Slide 67: ANCIEN PASSAGE

John Auldjo, a Scottish gentleman who later became British Consul in Geneva, published an illustrated account of his ascent of the mountain.

Mr John Auldjo, who went up Mont Blanc on Aug 9th 1827, says he crossed the Grand Plateau towards the left, 'leaving the old route, which led right across the plain'; and later on, when above the Rochers Rouges, he mentions that he 'came again into the old line of ascent, which we had quitted on the Grand Plateau' and says that the new line was first taken 'by Messrs Hawes and Fellowes, on the 25th July last.'

Auldjo left this remarkable drawing of a snow-bridge, and the following description: 'We were surrounded by ice piled up in mountains, crevices presenting themselves at every step, and masses half sunk in some deep gulf; the remainder, raised above us, seemed to put insurmountable barriers to our proceeding, yet some part was found where steps could be cut with the hatchet; and we passed over these bridges often grasping the ice with one hand, while the other, bearing the pole, balanced the body, hanging over some abyss into which the eye penetrated and searched in vain for the extremity. Sometimes we were obliged to climb up from one crag of ice to another; sometimes to scramble along a ledge on our hands and knees; often descending into a deep chasm on the one side, and scaling the slippery precipice on the other.'

Slide 68: AULDJO'S SNOW-BRIDGE

Slide 69: ACTUAL SNOW-BRIDGE ON MONT BLANC

Whymper's 1894 picture of a snow-bridge, though less dramatic than Auldjo's drawing, gives a good impression of members of the party putting their trust in the load-bearing qualities of compacted snow.

Aloys Pollinger, one of Whymper's guides on the 1894 expedition, had made more than 100 ascents of the Matterhorn. This staged picture gives an idea of the danger posed by hidden crevasses.

Slide 70: POLLINGER BREAKS THROUGH

Dr J Janssen, the present President of the French Academy of Sciences, and Director of the Observatory at Meudon near Paris, visited the Vallot Observatory a few weeks after it was put up [1890], to carry on spectroscopic observations. He was detained there several days by violent storms, but he ultimately ascended to the summit of Mont Blanc, and got back to Chamonix in safety. The journey occupied him from August 17 to August 23. He was struck with the advantages to science which might be expected from working in a pure atmosphere, and on his return to Paris communicated an account of his journey to the Academy of Sciences, at the meeting on September 22, 1890. He concluded by saying, 'I think it will be of the first importance for astronomy, for physics, and for meteorology that an observatory should be erected on the summit, or at least quite close to the summit, of Mont Blanc. I know that objections will be brought forward as to the difficulty of erecting such a building upon so high a spot, which one can only reach with much trouble, and which is often visited by tempests. These difficulties are real, but they are not insurmountable. I cannot enter deeply into the matter now, and content myself with saying that with the means our engineers can put at our disposal, and with such mountaineers as we possess at Chamonix and in the neighbouring valleys, the problem will be solved whenever we wish.' From that time until now Dr Janssen has been more or less occupied in solving the problem.

Slide 72: PORTRAIT OF DR JANSSEN

In a very short time the necessary funds were subscribed by some of his wealthy and influential friends. The execution of the project was a work of much greater difficulty. There is no visible rock at the immediate top and it was proposed to build upon the *snow*. This idea was received with almost universal incredulity.

Monsieur Eiffel, of Tower fame, was taken into consultation, and declared himself ready to construct an observatory on the very top of Mont Blanc, if a rock foundation could be found not more than fifty feet below the surface of the snow.

Slide 73: DRAGON APPEARS AGAIN

Slide 74: JANSSEN ASCENDING

Anyone seeing from a distance the great Dr Janssen being carried up the mountain might have thought that the fabled dragons had returned!

Dr Janssen has shewn an energy, courage, and tenacity in the prosecution of his undertaking which would be remarkable in anyone, and are doubly so in a man of threescore and ten, who is unable to climb a yard, and is so badly lame as to walk with difficulty even on level ground. Three times already he has had himself dragged to the summit in a sledge. On the second occasion the strength of his men was economised on steep places by using the windlasses which had already been employed to haul the materials.

Slide 75: DEPOT ON THE ROCHERS ROUGES

The peaks ranged around the Talèfre Glacier on the far side of the Mer de Glace – the Aiguilles Verte, Droites, Courtes and Triolet, with Mont Dolent beyond – are seen north-eastwards from the 1893 depot on the Petits Rochers Rouges (4577m/15,016ft): an interesting viewpoint.

In the winter of 1891-2 the Observatory (partly of iron and partly of wood) was constructed at Meudon, was taken to pieces and forwarded to Chamonix, and in the course of the latter year was transported up the mountain, under the management of Frédéric Payot. By the end of the season as about one quarter of the materials had been advanced to a little patch of rocks (the Petits Rochers Rouges) 750 feet below the summit, and the rest as far as the Grands Mulets. There they remained for the winter. The early part of 1893 was occupied in recovering the depot at the Petits Rochers Rouges, which was buried under 25 feet of snow, and in bringing up the remainder of the materials.

The Rochers Rouges, with Janssen's hut perched on the top and the Ancien Passage above to the right, from the vicinity of the Vallot Hut.

Taken from the Bosses Arête looking eastwards across the northern slopes below the summit of Mont Blanc, this picture shows the ice ramp of the Ancien Passage Supérieur with the crags of the Rochers Rouges Supérieurs below and Janssen's hut perched on the apex of the rocks at 4506m/14,783ft.

Slide 71: THE JANSSEN HUT ON THE ROCHERS ROUGES

The hut on the Rochers Rouges was constructed to support the exploratory tunnelling and the construction work for the Janssen observatory.

By the end of 1893, the building was erected on the summit, its heavier portions having been hauled up the terminal slope of snow, called the Calotte, by means of little windlasses, such as Payot is holding in the accompanying picture. The building, however, was not completed until the end of 1894.

EW and the Payot brothers were old friends.

M. Frédéric Payot earned my gratitude in 1865, by volunteering his assistance at a time when I was placed in a great difficulty. Since then he has risen to be Guide Chef thrice, and has ascended Mont Blanc more than a hundred times. His brother Michel shewed his capacity at an early age, and has, I believe, made more 'first ascents' in the Range of Mont Blanc than any other guide on the register.

Slide 88: FREDERIC PAYOT

When I visited it in July of that year it was more than half filled with snow, and two days of hard work were employed before it became tenantable.

Slide 83: ZURBRIGGEN EMERGING

The nearly complete observatory is seen here in 1894 with the 'edicule' beside it.

Slide 81: EXTERIOR OF OBSERVATORY

After a tunnel had failed to reach rock at the summit, Dr. Janssen decided to build his observatory on the snow.

Two important questions, he admitted, required first of all to be elucidated. One was, Will the observatory, if placed on the summit snow, sink or swim? The other was, What movements are there to dread in this snowy cap? To obtain an answer to the first question an experiment was carried out at Meudon. A column of lead weighing 792 lbs., but only one foot in diameter, was placed on piled up snow, brought to the density of that at the summit. The lead is said to have sunk in less than an inch, and Dr. Janssen considered this result encouraging. "As to the question of the movements," he said, "it was studied and determined by the installation in 1891 of a wooden edifice, which has now been two years on the spot." This edifice, which they term "the edicule" has now been in position for two years, but I do not feel that it has yet settled the 'question', [the point being that] the snows at the top of Mont Blanc are constantly descending to feed and maintain the glaciers below. The summit in 1891 was not the summit in 1892, nor will that of any succeeding year be the summit at a later date. The height of the mountain, nevertheless, remains nearly

Slide 82: INTERIOR OF OBSERVATORY

constant by the accession of fresh snow. It is not the liability of sinking into the snow, but the strong probability that any building erected on the top will sink with the snow, which gives rise to apprehension about the stability and maintenance of Dr. Janssen's Observatory. At the close of 1897, I was told it shewed marked signs of subsidence.

The principal instrument for the Observatory is termed a *Météorographe*, and has been constructed by Richard of Paris at a cost of £750. It registers barometric pressure, maximum and minimum temperatures, the direction and force of the wind etc, etc. It is put in movement by a weight of 200 lbs., which descends about 20 feet and is calculated to keep everything going for eight months – the length of time during which it is contemplated it may sometimes be left to itself.

In introducing his huge instrument to the Academy of Sciences on August 13, 1894, Dr. Janssen said, 'I do not conceal from myself that, notwithstanding the minute precautions which have been taken, there must be some degree of uncertainty about the result.'

In 1909, two years after Janssen's death, a crevasse opened up under the observatory and it was abandoned.

Within a short time, no trace remained of Dr. Janssen's observatory, though the Vallot Refuge and its successors, constructed on solid rock in 1890 just below the Bosses du Dromédaire at 4267m/14,320ft, has saved many lives over the years. The tragedy EW describes here would probably not have occurred if the Refuge had been available.

Slide 78: GRAVE OF McCORKINDALE

Engraving of Vallot refuge in 1895

This picture of the grave of the Rev. George McCorkindale at Chamonix is a poignant reminder of the dangers associated with high mountains. With two Americans, three guides and five porters, he was one of a party who all perished on Mont Blanc in September 1870, caught by appalling weather near the summit.

One of the Americans, a Mr Bean, left a notebook recording their final hours.

'Tuesday, September 6. I have made the ascent of Mont Blanc with ten persons; eight guides, Mr McCorkindale and Mr Randall. We arrived at the summit at half-past two. Immediately after leaving it I was enveloped in clouds of snow. We passed the night in a grotto excavated out of the snow, affording very uncomfortable shelter, and I was ill all night.
Mont Blanc, September 7. If any one finds the note-book, I beg that it may be sent to Mrs H M Bean, Jonesborough, Tennessee, United States of America.
My dear Hessie, - We have been on Mont Blanc for two days in a terrible snowstorm. We have lost our way and are in a hole scooped out of the snow at a height of 15,000 feet. I have no hope of descending. Perhaps this book may be found and forwarded. We have no food; my feet are already frozen, and I am exhausted; I have only strength to write a few words. I die in the faith of Jesus Christ, with affectionate thoughts of my family; my remembrances to all. My effects are in part at the Hotel Mont Blanc, and partly with me in two portmanteaux. Send them to the Hotel Schweitzerhof at Geneva; pay my bills at the hotel, and heaven will reward your kindness.'
And lower down, in nearly illegible writing:
'Morning. Intense cold; much snow, which falls uninterruptedly; guides restless.'

Slide 79: AGUILLE VERTE

Shot with a long-focus lens across the Arve valley from the vicinity of La Flégère, this picture shows the North West or Nant Blanc Face of the Aiguille Verte (4122m/13,524ft), a mountain of which EW made the first ascent – from the far side – just two weeks before his fateful Matterhorn climb of 1865. The rocky tooth of the Aiguille du Dru (3754m/12,316ft) was first climbed in 1878 by Clinton Dent's party – also from the far side – though the formidable North Face, seen here, remained unclimbed until long after EW's day.

I have already spoken of the disappointing nature of purely panoramic views. That seen from Mont Blanc itself is notoriously unsatisfactory. When you are upon that summit you look down upon all the rest of Europe. There is nothing to look up to; all is below; there is no one point for the eye to rest upon. The man who is there is somewhat in the position of one who has attained all he desires, - he has nothing to aspire to; his position must needs be unsatisfactory. Upon the summit of the Verte there is not this objection. You see valleys, villages, fields; you see mountains interminable rolling away, lakes resting in their hollows; you hear the tinkling of the sheep-bells as it rises through the clear mountain air, and the roaring of the avalanches as they descend to the valleys: but above all there is the great white dome, with its shining crest high above; with its sparkling glaciers that descend between buttresses which support them; with its brilliant snows, purer and yet purer the farther they are removed from this unclean world.

In 1865, Whymper made an ascent of the Grandes Jorasses, not least to obtain a view of the upper part of the Aiguille Verte, and this, in turn, required a viewpoint to determine the route.

The view here is not from Mont Saxe, but from the very summit of Mont Blanc. We look eastwards over the Col de Rochefort and the Aiguille du Géant to the Grands Jorasses (4208m/13,806ft), first climbed by EW, but only to the 24m/79ft lower West Summit, in 1865. Beyond, the Swiss Pennine Alps stretch into the distance, past the Grand Combin, to the Matterhorn, visible on the horizon over 40 miles/65 km away.

Slide 80: GRANDES JORASSES

My guides and I were reposing upon the top of Mont Saxe, scanning the Grandes Jorasses, with a view to ascending it. Five thousand feet of glacier-covered precipices rose above us, and up all that height we tracked a way to our satisfaction. Three thousand feet more of glacier and forest-covered slopes lay beneath, and there, there was only one point at which it was doubtful if we should find a path. The glaciers were shrinking, and were surrounded by bastions of rounded rock, far too polished to please the rough mountaineer. We could not track a way across them. However, at 4 a.m. the next day, under the dexterous leading of Michel Croz, we passed the doubtful spot. Thence it was all plain sailing, and at 1 p.m. we gained the summit. The weather was boisterous in the upper regions, and storm-clouds driven before the wind, and wrecked against our heights, enveloped us in misty spray, which danced around and fled away, which cut us off from the material universe, and caused us to be, as it were, suspended between heaven and earth, seeing both occasionally, but seeming to belong to neither.

Slide 84: MOTIONLESS EXPANSE OF CLOUDS

In July 1893 EW spent a night in the partly built observatory and then had the privilege of watching the sunrise from the highest vantage point in the Alps.

So high and massive is Mont Blanc that the vast but rapidly shrinking shadow it casts reaches far, far out onto the cloud sea that so often shrouds the Prealps of Savoie.

A vast sea of cloud lay motionless over the Italian valleys north of the valley of Aosta and all the peaks absolutely clear. I promenaded the ridge, looking right and left, sweeping the vast circumference to watch the development. The sun rose with a bound behind the Mischabel; Monte Rosa was in shadow but the other great peaks broke out like watchfires. Rays streamed through the openings between the peaks. Shortly after the sun was fairly risen the shadow of Mont Blanc was seen projected in the air in the direction of Aix-les-Bains. It was at first grey in tone, and might have been mistaken for another mountain; it deepened, and then sank and died away. The air was still and intensely cold.

This picture must have been taken before the construction of the observatory.

Slide 86: THE SUMMIT OF M.BLANC

The Summit has been described by various authors as resembling the back of a donkey, a pear cut in half, and the back of a carp. I am unable to account for these aberrations of intellect. The summit is a ridge of snow 145 paces long, descending more steeply on the French than upon the Italian side. Its crest is nearly level, but the eastern is slightly higher that the western end. There is every probability that three rocky ridges meet almost immediately underneath the Observatory, and at no great distance below it. The little patch of rock on the Italian side called la Tourette is only 171 feet lower than the very highest point. The summit of Mont Blanc de Courmayeur lies in the same direction, and can be visited in a short hour. Rope should be employed. The condition of the snow on the very top of Mont Blanc is usually good. The greater part of that which falls is blown or drifted away, and the small amount that remains behind speedily binds to the old snow underneath.

Slide 85: MONT BLANC FROM THE SUMMIT OF MONT BLANC DE COURMAYEUR

The summit of Mont Blanc de Courmayeur is about 600 metres to the south of the summit of Mont Blanc and roughly 250 metres lower.

In this picture, which must have been taken in 1894 or later, the Janssen Observatory occupies a prominent position on the skyline.

Paul Breton was the young man who carried the cameras on the 1894 expedition: another staged picture showing the very real danger posed by hidden crevasses.

Slide 87: PAUL IN A CREVASSE

Though there are not at the present time any visible crevasses close to the summit, a few years ago it was intersected by a rather considerable one, which rendered it difficult to go from one end to another.

Whymper here pays tribute to another great guide:

Who is Melchior Anderegg? Those who ask the question cannot have been in Alpine Switzerland, where the name of Melchior is as well known as the name of Napoleon. Melchior, too, is an Emperor in his way - a very Prince among guides. His empire is amongst the 'eternal snows,' - his sceptre is an ice-axe.

Melchior Anderegg, more familiarly, and perhaps more generally known simply as Melchior, was born at Zaun, near Meiringen, on April 6, 1828. He was first brought into public notice in Hinchcliffe's *Summer Months among the Alps*, and was known to very few persons at the time that little work was published. In 1855 he was 'Boots' at the Grimsel Hotel, and in those days, when he went out on expeditions, it was for the benefit of his mater, the proprietor. Melchior himself only got the *trinkgelt.*

Slide 89: MELCHIOR ANDEREGG (1828 - 1912)

Slide 90: MELCHIOR ANDEREGG IN OLD AGE

The debt owed by the early British mountaineers to their French, Italian and Swiss guides was incalculable, and we have already heard how Michel Croz was killed after the first ascent of the Matterhorn.

In 1856 he migrated to the Schwarenbach Inn on the Gemmi, where he employed his time in carving objects for sale. In 1858 he made numerous expeditions with Messrs. Hinchcliffe and Stephen, and proved to his employers that he possessed first-rate skill, indomitable courage, and an admirable character. His position has never been doubtful since that year, and for a long time there has been no guide whose services have been more in request: he is usually engaged a year in advance.

It would be almost an easier task to say what he has not done than to catalogue his achievements. Invariable success attends his arms: he leads his followers to victory, but not to death. I believe no accident has ever befallen travellers in his charge. Like his friend Almer, he can be called a safe man. It is the highest praise that can be given to a first-rate guide.

This is the huge East or Macugnaga Face of Monte Rosa, a formidable mountain wall some 2300m/7,500ft in height and virtually Himalayan in scale. Monte Rosa is actually a massif of nine separate four thousand metre summits, including the Dufourspitze, at 4634m/15,203ft, the third highest in the Alps. Although several of the lesser summits had already been ascended, the Dufourspitze was first reached by Charles Hudson – later killed on the first ascent of the Matterhorn – and his party in 1855. The Swiss flanks of the massif are rather less ferocious.

Slide 91: MONTE ROSA FROM THE MORO PASS

The recollections of past pleasures cannot be effaced. Even now, as I write, they crowd up before me. First comes an endless series of pictures, magnificent in form, effect and colour. I see the great peaks, with clouded tops, seeming to mount up for ever and ever; I hear the music of distant herds, the peasant's Jodel, and the solemn church bells; and I scent the fragrant breath of the pines: and after these have passed away, another train of thoughts succeeds - of those who have been upright, brave and true; of kind hearts and bold deeds; and of courtesies received at stranger hands, trifles in themselves, but expressive of that good will towards men which is the essence of charity.

Still, the last, sad memory hovers round, and sometimes drifts across like floating mist, cutting off sunshine, and chilling the remembrance of happier times. There have been joys too great to be described in words, and there have been griefs upon which I have not dared to dwell; and with these in mind I say, Climb if you will, but remember that courage and strength are nought without prudence, and that a momentary negligence may destroy the happiness of a lifetime. Do nothing in haste; look well to each step; and from the beginning think what may be the end.

EDWARD WHYMPER, CHAMONIX 1910
(born London 27 April 1840, died Chamonix 12 September 1911)

Guido Rey:

I was descending from the Theodul. Half-way between the Col and the Jomein I saw coming slowly up towards me a fine, tall old man, with a ruddy countenance, clean-shaven, clear-eyed, and with snowy-white hair. His face bore the impress of an iron will; his body straight as a dart notwithstanding his years, was full of vigour; his long, rhythmical gait testified to his familiarity with mountains. As I passed him I took off my hat to him, as is the polite custom of those who meet in the mountains. My guide whispered 'Do you know who that is?' I answered that I did not. 'Monsieur Whymper!' He had stopped and was looking at the Matterhorn, whose aspect was one of marvellous grandeur at that point.

I cannot describe how much I was impressed by that meeting in that spot. It was not a man I saw, but the idealized image of the perfect mountaineer, whom I and others have so often dreamed of imitating. They were there, the Matterhorn and Whymper, the two great rivals, and the sight of them in each other's presence brought home to one the superiority of the tiny conqueror to the conquered giant. He had come back after thirty years to see once more the mountain that had made him famous.

Sources

Edward Whymper:
Scrambles amongst the Alps in the years 1860-69, Murray 1871
Travels amongst the Great Andes of the Equator, Murray 1891-2
Chamonix and the Range of Mont Blanc, Murray 1896
The Valley of Zermatt and the Matterhorn, Murray 1897
Diaries 1860-1911 MS Scott Polar Research Institute Cambridge
ed. Ian Smith: *The Apprenticeship of a Mountaineer:* Edward Whymper's London Diary 1855-1859

Auldjo, John: *Narrative of an ascent to the Summit of Mont Blanc,* Longman 1827
Coolidge, W.A.B.: *The Alps in Nature and History*, Methuen 1908
Forbes, J.D.: *The Tour of Mont Blanc*, Black 1855
Irving, R.L.G.: *The Alps*, Batsford 1939
Mummery, A.F.: *My Climbs in the Alps and Caucasus,* Fisher Unwin 1895
Rey, Guido: *The Matterhorn*, Fisher Unwin 1907
Smith, Albert: *The Story of Mont Blanc*, Bogue 1853
Smythe, F.S.: *Edward Whymper*, Hodder and Stoughton 1940
Tyndall, John: *The Glaciers of the Alps*, Murray 1860